Living a worthy Life

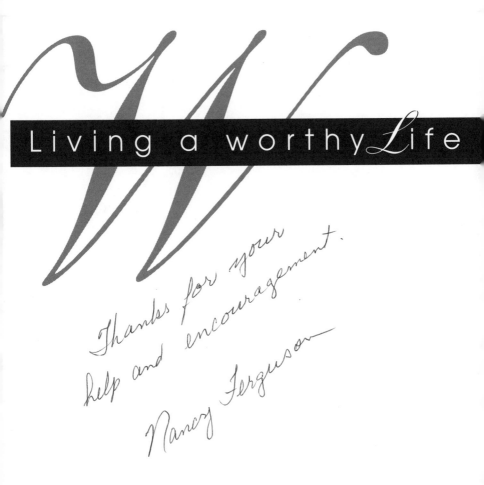

Living a worthy Life

*Thanks for your
help and encouragement.
Nancy Ferguson*

Nancy Ferguson

GOSPEL ADVOCATE COMPANY
P.O. BOX 150
NASHVILLE, TENNESSEE 37202

Published by Gospel Advocate Co.
P.O. Box 150, Nashville, TN 37202
http://www.gospeladvocate.com

ISBN: 0-89225-379-7

Dedication

To the memory of my parents, Byrd Ray and Lucile Walls Lewis, who taught me both by word and by example the value of living a worthy life.

And to my husband, Everett, who throughout our life together has demonstrated over and over what it is to live a worthy life.

*T*able of Contents

$\mathcal{P}$reface

$\mathcal{L}$iving a worthy life. Surely that is an admirable ambition for any Christian. But how do we do it? Do we even know what a worthy life is?

This book is written with a firm conviction that the Bible is the Word of God and that it is relevant for us today. Therefore, we want to see what the Bible says about the worthy life God wants each of us to live. We want to explore some areas in which a better understanding of biblical teachings will help us to live worthily. Although these few chapters will not be exhaustive, perhaps they will be thought provoking.

Some of these topics are misunderstood because we have not read the Bible enough, not because the teachings are difficult or disputed. Thus, there will be many Scripture quotations. By studying various verses on the same subject, we can better know God and His will for us. Definitions of crucial words will help clarify our perceptions.

Even those who understand the basic meaning of these concepts may have missed the deeper, richer significance. The better we comprehend God's message, the more meaningful our relationship with Him becomes. As we study God's Word we are drawn closer to Him.

Unless otherwise identified, quotations from the Bible are from the New International Version. Italics are used to indicate the translation of the Greek word under discussion. Transliterations of Greek words are also printed in italics.

Without the encouragement and help of my husband, this book would never have been written. His wisdom and understanding have guided me in many instances. His knowledge of the Scriptures has assisted me in my efforts to remain as true as possible to the Word of God. If I have erred, however, it is my misunderstanding, not his.

I am also indebted to Dr. Ed Coates and Dr. Jane Coates for their careful reading of the manuscript and for their most helpful suggestions.

$\mathcal{W}$orthy! Who, Me?

"[L]ive a life worthy of the Lord" (Colossians 1:10).

$\mathcal{H}$ave you ever felt that your life is a puzzle – a giant, complicated, overwhelming jigsaw puzzle? What do you do with all the pieces? How do you put it all together? Where do you start?

With Eyes on the Ideal

When working a jigsaw puzzle, it helps to know what the finished picture is supposed to be. If you can see that ideal picture, then you can compare the jumbled pieces with it and begin to see how they fit together. Some areas of the puzzle may be easy, so you will start there. Other areas will be so difficult that you would be glad to have some assistance. As you continue to work, referring often to the ideal, you see progress as the picture gradually comes together and makes sense. When pieces fit properly, you are elated.

The more pieces that fit together, the less complicated the rest of the puzzle becomes. Although some areas will remain hard, keeping close watch on what the picture is supposed to be will make putting the puzzle together easier. Unfortunately, sometimes crucial pieces are missing, and you are frustrated when the picture cannot be completed. Other times, something happens that upsets what has already been done – some-

11

one bumps the table, and it spills, or the cat walks across the puzzle and knocks it apart. Then you must start over again. Life can be like that jigsaw puzzle. We are surrounded by broken pieces, and we do not know how to put them together. We need a picture, an ideal, something to show us how our lives are supposed to be. If we can just see what God wants for us – how He wants us to live our lives – it will help us put our individual puzzles together. God has given us that ideal, if we will only look at it. In the Bible we find the ideal picture of what is best for us and how to live a worthy life.

Read the Bible

The purpose of this book is to help you see something of the worthy life that God wants you to live. To see this you must read the Bible. To make it easier, a number of scriptures on related topics have been brought together in each chapter. Do not take someone else's word for what is in the Bible. There is no substitute for looking at the perfect picture for yourself as you try to fit together the pieces of your own life.

Perhaps reading the Bible is difficult for you because you are using a translation that is hard to understand. The King James Version is written in beautiful English, but it is not what is spoken today. The out-of-date language sometimes obscures the meaning.

No single translation is the best. Reading from several different versions often helps us better understand the meaning of the Hebrew or Greek. Several standard translations are good, such as the New International Version; the New King James Version, written in more contemporary language than the 1611 version; the New Revised Standard Version; the New American Standard Bible; and the Easy-to-Read Version, written on a third-grade level and especially good for children to read for themselves.

Sometimes we approach the Bible assuming we cannot understand it. We look for someone smarter, wiser or more knowledgeable to tell us what the Bible says. However, the Bible was not written only for theologians and intellectuals. It was written in the common language of the time rather than in a formal literary style.

The Bible is for everyone. If you have the ability to read a novel and follow it or to read the newspaper and learn what it says, you can read the Bible. The important thing is to read it. Of course, you will find some things that are difficult to understand. There is enough depth and richness in the Bible that one can study it for a lifetime and still not know everything in it. However, most of the Bible is understandable to most people. Try it and see!

To Know God

We study the Bible not simply to know what it says but also to know God. If we do not know God, we cannot live worthy lives. Knowing Him makes us act better. Our hearts must be open to His will so that we can live His way. It is essential to keep His ideal before us at all times.

We may feel that this ideal is too perfect for us to attain. We see the picture in the Bible of complete worthiness, and we know we can never measure up to that – our own jigsaw puzzles are always missing some crucial pieces. The ideal of perfection is beyond our human capabilities of achievement. However, without seeing the goal we cannot even begin to put the puzzles of our lives together. We are sinners, but that does not mean we have to behave like sinners! God really does want something better for us than that. He is willing and able to help us, if we will just let Him, and if we will do what we can to live worthily.

Living Worthily

In several places the Bible urges us to "live a life worthy of" something: "the calling you have received" (Ephesians 4:1), "the gospel of Christ" (Philippians 1:27), "the Lord" (Colossians 1:10), and "God" (1 Thessalonians 2:12).

What does it mean to live a worthy life? In these verses the Greek word translated "worthy" is the adverb form of the word, not an adjective. It describes how we act, not what we are. A literal translation would be "live worthily." It does not mean that we ourselves have to be worthy; rather that we have to act in a worthy manner.

What "Worthy" Means

Now, what does the word "worthy" mean? Does it mean that we have to be perfect, that we always have to do the right thing, that we can never make any mistakes? That is what some people think, but is that correct?

The Greek word that is used in these verses is *axios*. It does not refer to perfection, but rather means to be appropriate to something. This word originally was used in connection with weights and balances. It referred to what was put on one end of a balance-type scale to bring the other end back up. Thus it meant being equivalent, counter-balancing or matching up with something else. The word came to refer to the relationship of balance between the objects on the two ends of the scale and was extended figuratively to people and things. It means appropriate to, corresponding to, consistent with, or in keeping with something.

The expression "the labourer is worthy of his hire" (Luke 10:7 KJV) does not mean that the worker has an exemplary character or that he is noble and righteous. Instead, it means that if the laborer does the job appropriately, it is right, fitting and proper that he should be paid. One side of the equation balances the other.

When we are told to live lives worthy of something, it means to act in a manner appropriate to that other component. Our actions should be consistent with, or corresponding to, the designated standard. We should try to be in balance with or live up to what is expected of us in the situation. We should behave fittingly.

Another way of saying "live worthily" is found in Galatians 5:25: "Since we live by the Spirit, let us keep in step with the Spirit." We should keep in step with the standard set by the Spirit and act in the way required by our relationship with the Spirit.

The negative form of the Greek word for "worthy" is used in 1 Corinthians 11:27 in giving instructions concerning the Lord's Supper: "Therefore, whoever eats the bread or drinks the cup of the Lord in an unworthy manner will be guilty of sinning against the body and blood of the Lord." This verse does not require that we be morally perfect and therefore worthy of participating in the Supper but rather that our manner of partaking should be in accord with what Christ has done for us.

Ephesians 5:3-4 defines another negative aspect of this concept by listing some activities that are improper and out of place for one who is trying to live worthily – sexual immorality, impurity, greed, obscenity, foolish talk or coarse joking. These are in contrast to the idea of fitting or appropriate behavior.

Before the Bible tells us to live worthy lives, it first describes what Christ has done for us and what tremendous power and glory are due Him. Only after this groundwork has been laid are we told how that knowledge should affect the way we live. Our morality grows out of our theology. We cannot know how to live unless we understand what God has told us to do. Thus in order to live a worthy life it is important to keep in mind the ideals found in the Bible.

Worthy of the Calling

In Ephesians we see something of what God has planned for us – what He has called us to be:

> I pray also that the eyes of your heart may be enlightened in order that you may know the hope to which he has called you, the riches of his glorious inheritance in the saints, and his incomparably great power for us who believe. (Ephesians 1:18-19)

> Because of his great love for us, God, who is rich in mercy, made us alive with Christ even when we were dead in transgressions ... that in the coming ages he might show the incomparable riches of his grace. ... For we are God's workmanship, created in Christ Jesus to do good works, which God prepared in advance for us to do. (2:4-9)

> Remember that formerly you who are Gentiles by birth ... were separate from Christ, ... without hope and without God in the world. But now in Christ Jesus you who once were far away have been brought near through the blood of Christ. (2:11-13)

God has called us to a great hope – the hope of heaven with its glorious riches. He has made us alive in order that we may do the good works He has planned for us. He has called us to share in the glories and riches that are in Christ.

In Ephesians 3 we are reminded of the grace of God, the unsearchable riches of Christ, the wisdom of God, the mighty power of the Spirit, and the great love Christ has for us. We are assured in verse 20 that God "is able to do immeasurably more than all we ask or imagine, according to his power that is at work within us" The prayer is that we may know the depth of the love that Christ has for us and be strengthened in our inner being with the fullness of God. We cannot even begin to imagine what power God has to help us. With His great power we are enabled to live worthy lives. But God will not do it for us – we must do our part. God calls us, but how do we answer?

Ephesians 4:1-3 tells us some of what our part is:

> I urge you to live a life worthy of the calling you have received. Be completely humble and gentle; be patient, bearing with one another in love. Make every effort to keep the unity of the Spirit through the bond of peace.

God has called us to be something better than what we used to be, better than the sinful world around us. Part of that some-thing better is being humble, gentle, patient, loving to one an-other, united in the Spirit, and peaceful. God has given us a lofty calling, and we should be true to that calling, making our conduct appropriate to it. Living up to our roles as Christians is an important motivation for the way we act.

How do we receive this calling from God? Second Thes-salonians 2:13-14 tells us that God wants us "to be saved through the sanctifying work of the Spirit and through belief in the truth. He called you to this through our gospel, that you might share in the glory of our Lord Jesus Christ." Because God's calling comes to us through the gospel, living a life wor-thy of the calling means living a life worthy of the gospel.

Worthy of the Gospel

When Paul wrote to the church in Philippi, he was in prison and on trial for his life for preaching the Word of God. He wanted to make sure that he would not be ashamed but that he would have the courage to do what he knew God wanted him to do (Philippians 1:20). He wanted to act in a manner worthy of the gospel of Christ, and he encouraged other Christians to do the same:

> Whatever happens, conduct yourselves in a manner worthy of the gospel of Christ. Then, whether I come and see you or only hear about you in my absence, I will know that you stand firm in one spirit, contending as one man for the faith of the gospel without being frightened in any way by those who oppose you. (vv. 27-28)

Living lives worthy of the gospel of Christ includes standing firm in one spirit, contending for the faith of the gospel, and not being frightened by those who oppose us. Thus we see that the gospel imposes certain responsibilities upon us as well as blessings. We need to conduct ourselves in a way that is in harmony with those responsibilities. We should act in a way that will not bring shame upon either ourselves or the gospel of Christ.

How do others know we are Christians? Is it not by the way we conduct our lives? Our faith in God must be shown by the things we do, the way we act, as well as by what we say. The way we live should be in agreement with the standard of the gospel of Christ.

Worthy of the Lord

Since the content of the gospel is Christ the Lord (1 Corinthians 15:1-8), living a life worthy of the gospel means living a life worthy of the Lord. The book of Colossians gives us some insights into how to live according to God's will. Paul wrote to the church at Colosse with thankfulness for their faith in Christ and their love for others. Their faith and love were grounded in the gospel of Christ. Again we hear about God's grace toward us. When we think of all that the Lord has done for us, our hearts overflow with gratitude and we want to please Him. The gospel the Colossians heard changed their lives even as that same gospel can change our lives. Colossians 1:9-14 urges us to live lives worthy of the Lord:

> For this reason, since the day we heard about you, we have not stopped praying for you and asking God to fill you with the knowledge of his will through all spiritual wisdom and understanding. And we pray this in order that you may live a life worthy of the Lord and may please him in every way: bearing fruit in every good work, growing in the knowledge of God, being strengthened with all power according to his glorious might so that you may have great endurance and patience, and joyfully giving thanks to the Father, who has qualified you to share in the inheritance of the saints in the kingdom of light. For he has rescued us from the dominion of darkness and brought us into the kingdom of the Son he loves, in whom we have redemption, the forgiveness of sins.

This passage lists several things that help us know how we may please God. Among them are doing good works, learning about God, being strengthened by His power, having endurance and patience, and giving thanks to God for all He has done for us.

We have the responsibility of trying to please God in everything we do. We must do what we can to live a worthy life, but it is the Father who enables us, who qualifies us, to do so. Without Him we cannot live a worthy life. He even helps us by supplying some of those missing pieces in the puzzles of our lives.

The gospel of Christ brings us to the Lord so that we can live a life worthy of God.

Worthy of God

In 1 Galatians, as in Colossians, we find that Paul is rejoicing and thanking God for the people to whom he is writing. They are imitating the Lord and are models for others. Yet, they are gently and tenderly encouraged to continue to live lives worthy of God.

> For you know that we dealt with each of you as a father deals with his own children, encouraging, comforting and urging you to live lives worthy of God, who calls you into his kingdom and glory.
> (1 Thessalonians 2:11-12)

Imagine that you are selected for some great honor. Probably everyone will look up to you and expect even greater things from you because of that honor. Would that influence the way you live, the way you act? Are there petty things in your life that you would want to eliminate? Would you be more careful in what you do? Would you want to do something to please those who selected you for that honor? Why? Because the situation would call for appropriate actions from you. If an earthly honor could cause you to act better, how much more should the heavenly honor of being called into God's kingdom and glory cause a change in your behavior!

Close your eyes and try to picture yourself actually being summoned into the presence of God. All human honors pale in comparison with the glory and honor of being called into His kingdom. What a wonderful, awe-inspiring thing it is that the almighty God in heaven, the Creator of the universe, the all-wise, loving Father, has asked us to share His kingdom and His glory! Surely that will affect the way we live our lives here on earth. Surely that will make us want to live lives worthy of such an honor and privilege.

To Please God

In 1 Thessalonians, we are urged not only to live lives worthy of God but also to live in order to please God. In 4:1-12 we find some instructions that will help us do this. Perhaps we will understand these instructions better if we list them in outline form.

I. It is God's will (verse 3):
    A. that you should be holy (v. 3)
    B. that you should avoid sexual immorality (v. 3)
    C. that you should learn to control your own body (v. 4)
        1. in a way that is holy and honorable and (v. 4)

2. not in passionate lust like the heathen, who do not
   know God (v. 5)
D. that no one should wrong others or take advantage
   of them (v. 6).

II. God did not call you to be impure but to live holy
    lives (v. 7):
   A. to love each other (v. 9)
   B. to lead a quiet life (v. 11)
   C. to mind your own business (v. 11)
   D. to work with your hands (v. 11)
   E. to win the respect of outsiders (v. 12)
   F. not to be dependent on anybody (v. 12)

It is important to see that these things are to be done in our
daily lives, not just on Sunday or other times when we happen
to think about God. In order to live a worthy life, a life consistent with the Lord, we have to live to please Him every day.

Another scripture that encourages us to please God and to
do His will is Ephesians 5:

> Live as children of light (for the fruit of the light
> consists in all goodness, righteousness and truth)
> and find out what pleases the Lord. (vv. 8-10)
>
> Be very careful, then, how you live – not as unwise
> but as wise, making the most of every opportuni-
> ty. … Therefore do not be foolish, but understand
> what the Lord's will is. Do not get drunk on wine,
> which leads to debauchery. Instead, be filled with
> the Spirit. Speak to one another with psalms,
> hymns and spiritual songs. Sing and make music
> in your heart to the Lord, always giving thanks to
> God the Father for everything, in the name of our
> Lord Jesus Christ.
> Submit to one another out of reverence for Christ.
> (vv. 15-21)

God's will for how we live is not a big mystery. These verses encourage us to find out what pleases God and then do it
carefully. It is foolish not to understand the Lord's will.
Drunkenness and other sins will keep us away from that un-

derstanding. Part of His will for us is that we should be good, righteous and truthful; that we should be happy and thankful.

Colossians 1:10 tells us not only to live worthily but also to please God in everything we do. "And we pray this in order that you may live a life worthy of the Lord and may please him in every way." Part of living a worthy life is pleasing the Lord. When we please Him, then the quality of our lives is better. Actually, when we please the Lord, we also please ourselves. The less sin we have in our lives, the better off we are.

It is also God's will for us to be joyful and thankful. "Be joyful always; pray continually; give thanks in all circumstances, for this is God's will for you in Christ Jesus" (1 Thessalonians 5:16-18). A person who is entangled in sin cannot have the joy God wants for us. The kind of joy meant here is not gleefulness and laughter all the time – it is much deeper than that. It is not dependent on what is happening around us but depends on our attitude toward those circumstances.

Living a worthy life does not mean that we are without problems or that we are exuberantly happy all the time. Contentment comes with knowing that we are doing our part and that God gives us the strength to face and conquer our problems, whatever they are. When we think of the power and glory of God, we feel a deep-down joy that makes us pray and give thanks in all circumstances. There is happiness in knowing that we do not have to solve all our problems by ourselves – we have help. Our lives will be much better if we cultivate the attitude of prayerfully expressing joy and thankfulness in everything. God really does want us to be happy, but the only way we can be *happy* is to be *holy*.

God Counts Us Worthy

To live worthily does not mean that by ourselves we must be, or even can be, worthy, but rather that with God's help we can and should live in a way that is appropriate to our being Christians. Even when we cannot live up to the ideal, God can still count us worthy, can still treat us as if we are worthy. This is the Good News that Christ came to bring to us.

Ephesians 1:3-4 emphasizes that we are blessed spiritually in Christ. "Praise be to the God and Father of our Lord Jesus

Christ, who has blessed us in the heavenly realms with every spiritual blessing in Christ. For he chose us in him before the creation of the world to be holy and blameless in his sight."

Worthy, Though Prodigal

God has always planned for His people to be holy and blameless in His sight. That He can see us this way even when we are not worthy is illustrated by the parable of the prodigal son beginning in Luke 15:11. The son took his inheritance and left home. He wasted his money and his opportunities. When nothing was left, he could only feed the pigs while he went hungry. He decided to go home.

When the son said, "I am no longer worthy to be called your son" (v. 19), he admitted his unworthiness. He knew that because of the many wrong things he had done he did not deserve to be treated as his father's son. Yet, as he approached home, his father saw him coming and ran to meet him (v. 20).

This loving father knew that his son had been living a sinful life, but he greeted him as befitting a well-loved and long-lost son. Although he did not approve of what his son had done, he still loved him. The father counted him worthy to be his son, even though he was not actually worthy. This devoted father cared so much for his sinful son that he saw only the son, not the sin. Even today this is the way God's children are holy and blameless in His sight.

Worthy by Grace

This worthiness is quite different from the concept of being worthy by actually earning or meriting that status. We cannot make a claim on God and say that we deserve anything from Him. Rather it is His grace that gives us the opportunity of fellowship with Him. Our worth is not determined by how good we are but by whether we have received the gospel of Christ and obeyed it; that is, if we are children of the Father. As the father put the robe, sandals and ring on the boy (Luke 15:22), so God clothes us with righteousness and gives us the sign of being His heir.

This son was not "good enough" to deserve his father's love, yet he was welcomed home. Sometimes those who are not yet Christians feel they must be "good enough" before they can become Christians. We all sometimes feel that we must get our lives together first, that we must prove to ourselves and to others that we are able to live the Christian life – only then can we approach God. We have missed the point. Without Christ, there is no way we can get our lives together. There is no way anyone can live a life worthy of the Lord without the Lord.

The point is that we bring our lives – broken, sinful and without hope – to Him. In doing that, we say, "Lord, I know I can't do it by myself. I know that You are the only One who has the power to straighten out the mess I've made of everything. Please help me. I turn myself over to You. I'm not worthy to be Your child, but here I am."

When we turn to God and obey Him, He heals us, He forgives us, He saves us, He enables us to live the kind of life He wants from us. He welcomes us home and helps us to fit together the pieces of our puzzles. This does not mean that suddenly we have no more problems and that everything is perfect. It means that God is there to help us solve our problems. With His help we will be able to pick up the pieces and begin to put them in their proper place.

Many passages of Scripture assure us of God's help and comfort. In Isaiah 41:10 God promises His care and support:

> So do not fear, for I am with you;
>   do not be dismayed, for I am your God.
> I will strengthen you and help you;
>   I will uphold you with my righteous right hand.

Anytime we are in any kind of trouble it is comforting to think about Psalm 46:1:

> God is our refuge and strength,
>   an ever-present help in trouble.

Because of the comfort and help we have from God, we are able to comfort others:

> Praise be to the God and Father of our Lord Jesus Christ, the Father of compassion and the God of all comfort, who comforts us in all our troubles, so that we can comfort those in any trouble with the

comfort we ourselves have received from God.
(2 Corinthians 1:3-4)

What a relief it is to know that we do not have to be perfect, that there is hope for us even when we fail as badly as the prodigal son! God knows we cannot be perfect, but He does want us to try our best to live the way that is right, the way that is in step with His way, that brings glory to Him. The son in the parable realized how wrong he was and returned to his father. We too have to turn our backs on sin and head ourselves in the right direction – the direction toward God and His worthiness. We have to keep the goal of a worthy life in front of us and do the things that are right.

Grace to Endure

Putting our puzzles together is a life-long process; thus, we cannot expect to be able to put all the pieces in place immediately. Sometimes we see progress; then something happens that tears the pieces apart and we have to start over again. No matter how many times this happens, God will still help us. Although we will never get it complete in this life, there is no excuse to give up. We must keep trying and keep making progress as we mature in the Lord. When we have done all we can, God will provide the rest of the pieces at the judgment.

Even the apostle Paul realized the importance of continuing to try to gain the righteousness that comes from God through faith in Christ.

> I want to know Christ and the power of his resurrection and the fellowship of sharing in his sufferings, becoming like him in his death, and so, somehow, to attain to the resurrection from the dead. Not that I have already obtained all this, or have already been made perfect, but I press on to take hold of that for which Christ Jesus took hold of me. Brothers, I do not consider myself yet to have taken hold of it. But one thing I do: Forgetting what is behind and straining toward what is ahead, I press on toward the goal to win the prize for which God has called me heavenward in Christ Jesus. (Philippians 3:10-14)

We ourselves are not worthy and cannot be worthy. Only God is truly worthy. "You are worthy, our Lord and God, to receive glory and honor and power, for you created all things, and by your will they were created and have their being" (Revelation 4:11).

We can never live up to the perfection that is God's, but that should not keep us from trying. Ultimately, God will make us like Him, but there are rewards in this life, too. By living the way God wants us to live, the quality of our lives on this earth will be much better. We need to have the goal of perfect holiness before us so that we know what we are aiming toward. Otherwise we do not know what we are doing.

According to 2 Thessalonians 1, God will help us by counting us worthy:

> We ought always to thank God for you, brothers, and rightly so, because your faith is growing more and more, and the love every one of you has for each other is increasing. Therefore, among God's churches we boast about your perseverance and faith in all the persecutions and trials you are enduring. (vv. 3-4)

> All this is evidence that God's judgment is right, and as a result you will be counted worthy of the kingdom of God, for which you are suffering. (v. 5)

> With this in mind, we constantly pray for you, that our God may count you worthy of his calling, and that by his power he may fulfill every good purpose of yours and every act prompted by your faith. (v. 11)

The passages exhorting us to live worthily show us the standard of what constitutes a worthy life: the Christian calling, the gospel, the Lord, and God. When we try to live up to this standard, then we are trying to be like God.

Imitate God

God wants us to be as much like Him as we can be. In Matthew 5:48 Jesus said, "Be perfect, therefore, as your heavenly Father is perfect." In the preceding verses Jesus taught

His disciples to love others, even their enemies. Showing god-like love to others is one way to be like the Father.

In 1 Peter 1:15-16 we read, "But just as he who called you is holy, so be holy in all you do; for it is written: 'Be holy, because I am holy.'" The motivation for trying to be holy is that God is holy, and He wants us to be like Him.

When we obey Christ and become a part of Him, we no longer think as we used to think; we have a new viewpoint. The sins that were important to us before are no longer important. However, Satan will be eager for the old thoughts to cross our minds again.

When we slip back into old habits, perhaps only momentarily, we may become discouraged. We may feel that if we cannot live up to expectations, we might as well give up and quit trying. The world tells us that living the Christian life is just too hard, and sometimes even fellow Christians tell us the same thing. Yet God wants us to continue to live worthy lives, and He will always be there to help us.

Ephesians 4:22-24 encourages us to continue living this new life in Christ:

> You were taught, with regard to your former way of life, to put off your old self, which is being corrupted by its deceitful desires; to be made new in the attitude of your minds; and to put on the new self, created to be like God in true righteousness and holiness.

We are "created to be like God in true righteousness and holiness" (v. 24). How do we live up to that? The verses that follow (4:25-5:2) give us some idea of what it means. Do not lie, but tell the truth; do not stay angry; do not let the devil get hold of you; do not steal, but do useful work for a living; share with the needy; watch your language, saying only things that are helpful to others; do not make God unhappy; get rid of wrong things in your lives; be nice to others; and forgive others. In other words, "[b]e imitators of God, therefore, as dearly loved children and live a life of love, just as Christ loved us and gave himself up for us as a fragrant offering and sacrifice to God" (5:1-2). Christians should behave as described in this passage because of our relationship to God.

To Reflect His Glory

God not only wants us to be like Him, but He also wants us to glorify Him in such a way that others will see His glory. "Live such good lives among the pagans that, though they accuse you of doing wrong, they may see your good deeds and glorify God on the day he visits us" (1 Peter 2:12). The purpose of living a worthy life is not just for ourselves, but for the benefit of others also.

Second Peter 3:11 tells us, "You ought to live holy and godly lives." As we continue to live holy and godly lives, we grow in love and understanding. Doing this is important not only for now, but also for the future.

> And this is my prayer: that your love may abound more and more in knowledge and depth of insight, so that you may be able to discern what is best and may be pure and blameless until the day of Christ, filled with the fruit of righteousness that comes through Jesus Christ – to the glory and praise of God. (Philippians 1:9-11)

God's Perfect Will

God wants what is best for us. His will is never bad for us. "Do not conform any longer to the pattern of this world, but be transformed by the renewing of your mind. Then you will be able to test and approve what God's will is – his good, pleasing and perfect will" (Romans 12:2).

If God's will is good, pleasing and perfect, our job should be to find out what His will is for us and then to do it. First Thessalonians 4:3 contains one of the simplest definitions of God's will. "It is God's will that you should be holy." Because God is holy, it follows that He wants us to be like Him.

God stands ready to give us all the help we need, but we must do our part. Hebrews 13:20-21 shows that God will help us do His will:

> May the God of peace, who through the blood of the eternal covenant brought back from the dead our Lord Jesus, that great Shepherd of the sheep, equip you with everything good for doing his will, and may he work in us what is pleasing to him,

through Jesus Christ, to whom be glory for ever and ever. Amen.

God wants us to do good, and thereby to influence others, as we learn from 1 Peter 2:15-16:

> For it is God's will that by doing good you should silence the ignorant talk of foolish men. Live as free men, but do not use your freedom as a cover-up for evil; live as servants of God.

In Ephesians 6:5-8 instructions are given to slaves, but those same instructions can apply to all of us. It is not enough just to go through the motions of obeying the will of God; we must obey from our hearts.

> Slaves, obey your earthly masters with respect and fear, and with sincerity of heart, just as you would obey Christ. Obey them not only to win their favor when their eye is on you, but like slaves of Christ, doing the will of God from your heart. Serve wholeheartedly, as if you were serving the Lord, not men, because you know that the Lord will reward everyone for whatever good he does, whether he is slave or free.

Why should we obey God's will? Because God's way is always the best way. When we decide that we want to do things His way, many things become easier for us. Those who do not know God may feel that living a worthy life is too hard, but it really is not, because God is with us and eases our burdens.

Some people think that if we only trust God, our lives here on earth will be perfect, easy, happy-go-lucky, trouble free, pain free, worry free, care free, problem free and hassle free. However, that is what heaven will be. Nevertheless, with God's help we can have the best quality of life possible on this earth. We will have the endurance to go on. We will have the guidance needed to make right decisions. It is the inner strength given by God that makes the difference. People who do not know God and thus do not trust Him do not have His power to sustain them. With God's help we can overcome anything the devil can throw at us.

Staying Aware of the Goal

Every golfer would like to shoot a perfect hole-in-one every time, but no one really expects to do so. However, one has a much better chance of success by keeping focused on the hole. If the golfer is not aware of the goal, the ball will not drop in the hole. After taking the first stroke, the golfer can see how the ball missed the hole. The goal is reassessed and the aim is corrected for the next shot. With every stroke the golfer looks toward the hole and wants to sink the ball on that shot. When the ball goes in a hole, then the next hole becomes the challenge. Although each tee shot may be accompanied by the wish for a hole-in-one, that wish probably will not be realized. Yet the golfer will keep trying. By continually trying to get the ball in that little hole, the golfer becomes better and better.

Life is like a game of golf. If we keep focused on the goal and keep aiming for the holiness and perfection that God wants for us, we get better and better at attaining our goals. There is one big difference between golf and life. As we are trying to live the kind of life God planned for us, He helps us. In golf the hole never moves over to swallow somebody's bad shot, and the ball does not veer abruptly to fall in the hole. However, in life God gives us an advantage. In James 4:8 He made a promise to us: "Come near to God and he will come near to you." In effect, when we try to do what He wants us to do, He will move our ball to help us hit the hole. In doing this He does not lower His standards for us, but like a magnet He pulls us toward Him to make us more like Him.

We can never live in such a way as to earn salvation, but our gratitude for what God has done for us through Christ should lead us to want to live worthily for Him.

Perhaps by studying more deeply the concepts explored in this book we will see better how to do this. We cannot apply a principle to our lives in practice until we understand that principle in theory. These principles are neither new nor difficult to understand. Misunderstanding them may be common today because so many voices have misquoted them that the true meaning has been forgotten. Only by checking the Source can we understand and apply these principles.

Discussion Questions

1. In what ways is your life like a jigsaw puzzle?
2. How has your life been impacted by studying the Bible?
3. What distinction do you see between "living worthily" and "being worthy"? How can God still count you worthy even when you do things that are sinful?
4. In order for you to live worthily, what needs to be changed in your life? Why? How can it be changed?
5. How do you feel about having a perfect ideal for which to strive? How does keeping this ideal in your mind help you live a worthy life?
6. What is the basis upon which you decide to live worthily? Why should you want to live a worthy life? What is the purpose of living a worthy life?
7. Describe the kind of life you think God wants for you. Why do you think that is what He wants?
8. How can you determine what God's will for your daily life really is? How can you incorporate these things into your life?
9. In what ways can and should you try to be like God? What specific things in your life will be affected by imitating God?

$\mathcal{H}$ow Much Obedience Do I Owe God?

"If you love me, you will obey what I command" (John 14:15).

"$\mathcal{T}$hat's just something Jesus wants us to do. You can do it if you want to, and if you don't want to, you don't have to."

That casual remark by a friend has disturbed me for many years. Is it a valid statement of principle, or is it a fallacy? Is obedience to God necessary, or is it optional? How can we know?

What Choice Do We Have?

God has always wanted His people to obey Him, but He has always given us the freedom to make our own decisions. If we obey Him, there are blessings; if we do not obey Him, there are consequences. In the garden of Eden, Adam and Eve knew what God wanted, but they were lured into disobedience and bore the punishment.

Choice in the Old Testament

Even though God selected the Israelites to be His designated people, He did not force them to obey Him. They were free to choose between God and idols. In Joshua 24 the Israelites presented themselves before God at Shechem. There Joshua reminded them of what God had done for them from

the time of Abraham and Terah until that time, emphasizing
His protection and guidance in leading them from Egypt.
Joshua tells the people:

> Now fear the Lord and serve him with all faithful-
> ness. Throw away the gods your forefathers wor-
> shiped beyond the River and in Egypt, and serve the
> Lord. But if serving the Lord seems undesirable to
> you, then choose for yourselves this day whom you
> will serve, whether the gods your forefathers served
> beyond the River, or the gods of the Amorites, in
> whose land you are living. But as for me and my
> household, we will serve the Lord. (vv. 14-15)

The people gave their answer in verse 18: "We too will serve
the Lord, because he is our God." They recognized the power and sovereignty of God as shown by His mighty actions in
bringing them out of Egypt. They chose Him over the pow-
erless idols of the people around them.

In verses 19 and 20, Joshua warned the people what would
happen if they rebelled against God:

> You are not able to serve the Lord. He is a holy
> God; he is a jealous God. He will not forgive your
> rebellion and your sins. If you forsake the Lord
> and serve foreign gods, he will turn and bring dis-
> aster on you and make an end of you, after he has
> been good to you.

Again the people insisted that they had chosen to serve the
Lord and would abide by that decision. In verses 23 and 24,
Joshua explained what serving the Lord meant. "'Now then,'
said Joshua, 'throw away the foreign gods that are among
you and yield your hearts to the Lord, the God of Israel.' And
the people said to Joshua, 'We will serve the Lord our God
and obey him.' "

Although God selected the Israelite nation for His own people, each individual had to decide whether to obey God or
not. Choosing to serve God meant yielding their hearts to
Him alone and obeying Him. Choosing not to obey Him
meant suffering the consequences that would surely follow.

Choice Today

The same is true today. We are free to decide if we will obey God. He does not force obedience on us. The Cross draws us to Christ; it does not drive us. If we choose to obey God, He will be with us, and we will enjoy His blessings. However, if we choose not to obey Him, then by default we choose the punishment of separation from God that goes with rebellion against Him. The choice is ours.

If we believe the promises of God enough to obey Him, then by the grace of God and the actions of Christ, we become pure, holy and blameless in His sight. Of course, we ourselves are not really pure, holy and blameless, but God chooses to see us that way. One of the many scriptures written to Christians that teach this concept is Colossians 1:21-23:

> Once you were alienated from God and were ene-
> mies in your minds because of your evil behavior.
> But now he has reconciled you by Christ's physical
> body through death to present you holy in his sight,
> without blemish and free from accusation – if you
> continue in your faith.

Galatians 3:27 says, "[F]or all of you who were baptized into Christ have been clothed with Christ." When God looks at Christians, He sees only Christ.

This same idea is also found in Colossians 3:3: "For you died, and your life is now hidden with Christ in God." If we are clothed with Christ and if our lives are hidden with Christ, then God looks at us and sees only the holiness of Christ.

This does not mean that we are sinless. Rather it means that God chooses to forgive us of our sins and reconcile us to Himself, as we learn from 2 Corinthians 5:19: "God was reconciling the world to himself in Christ, not counting men's sins against them. And he has committed to us the message of reconciliation."

The way God looks at us is what ultimately counts. When we are in Christ and God looks at us to judge us, He chooses to see Christ and His holiness instead of our vileness. We are, in effect, hiding behind Christ. It is His purity, not ours, that God sees and that will save us.

God sees us the same way the father in the parable of the prodigal son (Luke 15:11-31) saw his son: because of the father's great love for the son and because of the son's repentant attitude, the father chose to see the son and not the sin. The father did not go after the son and force him to come home; the son had to come to the father by his own choice.

Although God chooses to see us as blameless, we will still be held accountable for our actions in this life. Like the son in the parable, we must come to the Father. When we turn our backs on sin and try to follow God's way, He will supply the missing pieces of the jigsaw puzzles of our lives.

Our Debt Has Been Fully Paid

How much obedience do we owe God? The answer is that we owe God nothing! That may be a startling statement, but it is what we learn from Colossians 2:13-14, which was written to those who were already Christians: "He forgave us all our sins, having canceled the written code, with its regulations, that was against us and that stood opposed to us; he took it away, nailing it to the cross."

Sometimes the "written code" discussed in this passage is understood to be the Law of Moses. However, the Law is not mentioned here. In other contexts Paul is careful to say "the law" when he means the Law of Moses. For example, in Romans 7:4-6 the Law is explicitly mentioned and refers to the Law of Moses:

> So, my brothers, you also died to the law through the body of Christ, ... we have been released from the law so that we serve in the new way of the Spirit, and not in the old way of the written code.

"Written code" in Romans 7:6 translates the Greek word, *gramma*, which means a letter, a writing, or a book – as the book of the Law. However, the Greek word translated "written code" in Colossians 2:14 is a different word, *cheirographon*. This word refers to a statement or certificate of indebtedness, a bond, or a handwritten document, as when one signs a note to make a purchase or pay back a loan. We could call it an IOU. Compare this definition with what Paul says in Philemon

18-19: "If he has done you any wrong or owes you anything, charge it to me. I, Paul, am writing this with my own hand. I will pay it back." Paul was signing a handwritten certificate promising to repay any debt that Onesimus owed Philemon.

The written code nailed to the cross was not the Law of Moses, instead it was the debt of sin that we owe. God took that IOU with its stipulations about what we owe, that promissory note outstanding against us that showed all our debts and that condemned us, and He nailed it to the cross. Christ paid the debt for us so we do not still **owe** it! He paid it all! God canceled that debt because of what Christ did for us on the cross. In God's eyes, we owe Him nothing. Although this seems to be a difficult concept, it may be easier to understand than to accept into our lives.

We Owe Nothing!

It was difficult for the unmerciful servant in the parable of the two debtors recorded in Matthew 18:21-34 to understand how his total forgiveness should affect his life. This servant owed his master an amount roughly equal to his salary for 150,000 years. Although the servant insisted that he would pay all of the debt, the king, knowing the impossibility of the situation, took pity on him, canceled the debt, and let him go. The servant owed his master absolutely nothing. So what did he do? He immediately went out, found someone who owed him about three months' salary, and demanded payment! Did he learn nothing from the actions of his master? He may have understood that he no longer owed the master anything, but he could not comprehend how that should influence his own behavior. He neither accepted nor gave forgiveness.

God has done for us what the master in the parable did for his servant. He has forgiven all our debt, even though our spiritual debt is much greater than the money owed by that servant. We *owe* nothing. God has completely forgiven us all our sins. Christ redeemed us – He bought us by His death on the cross. We are thus no longer slaves to sin, for now we belong to Him and are free to choose to obey Him instead of being enslaved by sin.

One reason the concept of owing nothing is difficult for us is because of the terminology we use. Although we say that we owe God nothing, in one sense we actually owe Him everything – the air we breath, the food we eat, our very lives. God provides everything for us. Without Him we would be absolutely nothing.

Yet, God does not demand payment from us for all He has done for us. God is not like the electric company – He gives us of His power freely and abundantly. He does not charge us. We owe the electric company; we do not owe God. Thus, when we say that we owe God nothing, we mean that the tremendous debt we have run up has been paid by someone else, and God does not require that we make installment payments on something that we could never repay.

A Free Gift

God has forgiven us an enormous debt, one that we could never repay. He has set us free from our debt of sin. He has given us a precious gift, and it is hard for us to realize the enormity of that gift. Focusing upon what God has done for us will help.

Many passages in the Bible tell us of His love, care and promises. Among them are the first two chapters of Ephesians. The whole passage is important, but a few selections are especially meaningful to this study. Notice the richness of the blessings described in 1:3-2:10:

> Praise be to the God and Father of our Lord Jesus Christ, who has blessed us in the heavenly realms with every spiritual blessing in Christ. For he chose us ... to be holy and blameless in his sight. ... In him we have redemption through his blood, the forgiveness of sins, in accordance with the riches of God's grace that he lavished on us ...
>
> I pray also that the eyes of your heart may be enlightened in order that you may know the hope to which he has called you, the riches of his glorious inheritance in the saints, and his incomparably great power for us who believe. ...
>
> But because of his great love for us, God, who is rich in mercy, made us alive with Christ even when we were dead in transgressions – it is by grace you

have been saved. And God raised us up with Christ and seated us with him in the heavenly realms in Christ Jesus, in order that in the coming ages he might show the incomparable riches of his grace, expressed in his kindness to us in Christ Jesus. For it is by grace you have been saved, through faith – and this not from yourselves, it is the gift of God – not by works, so that no one can boast. For we are God's workmanship, created in Christ to do good works, which God prepared in advance for us to do.

When we look at the abundance of the blessings God has for us, how can we say we owe him nothing? Because Ephesians 2:8 tells us that "it is the gift of God." One does not owe someone else for a gift. God is not engaged in the social exchange of presents or obligations. He offers a free gift.

Have you ever done someone a favor, not because you had to, or ought to, or because you wanted something from that person, but just because you loved him or her and wanted to do something special, with no strings attached?

Perhaps you have given a small child a present even though there was no special occasion. It was simply a gift of love. You did not expect anything in return from that child, but you were pleased to see the delight on the child's face as the gift was accepted. The joyful, appreciative attitude of a grateful child may be one of the reasons that God says we should become like little children before we can enter the kingdom of heaven.

A story published in a popular magazine a few years ago may help us understand the concept of a free gift. It was about a milkman who delivered milk to the home of a woman who had several young children. Her husband was out of work, and she was often behind in her payments. The family moved while still owing the milkman nearly $100.

At first the milkman was resentful and felt that the family had cheated him. However, he later began to think about the situation in a different light. To make himself feel better, he thought about the children who would have gone hungry without the milk he delivered even though he was not paid for it. He decided that he would consider the milk as a gift to the family. By doing this he no longer was bitter but found peace with himself. He felt good that he had been able to help someone else.

Some time later the milkman happened to meet the lady, who apologized for moving in such a hurry that she was unable to let him know where they were. She now had the money and tried to repay the debt that she owed him. However, the milkman refused the money, insisting that she did not owe him anything because he had given the milk to her family. He gave her a free gift; she no longer owed him anything. He expected no payment at all from her.

The concept of a free gift is hard for us to grasp. We often hear Christians say such things as:

"Every Christian ought to be involved in these certain activities."

"A good Christian would not do this particular activity."

"A good Christian ought to act in this specified way."

Some people try to make us feel guilty for not doing their pet projects. Certainly many deeds will not get done unless Christians become involved. However, guilt should never be the motivating factor for doing what is right. There are times when we should feel guilty – when we have done something wrong – but when God forgives us, we must accept it. We should not carry around a load of guilt after He has forgiven us. Nor should we use the idea of "owing God" as a way of laying a burden of guilt on people in order to get them to do what we want them to do.

We are sometimes like the debtor in the parable. He was forgiven thousands of years' worth of salary, then tried to make the second debtor repay him a few months' salary. God has forgiven us a heavy burden of sin, but too often we find it difficult to forgive even a minor offense by someone else.

We do not owe God anything – He has given us the glorious gift of redemption and freedom!

Too Good to Be True?

In this world, if something seems too good to be true, it probably is too good to be true. However, with God it is different. He does immeasurably more for us than we can even imagine (Ephesians 3:20-21). It is extremely difficult for us to understand what a free gift really is. We assume that if someone gives us something, there must be strings attached. If someone gives us a Christmas gift, we feel obligated to buy that person something, whether we had intended to do so or not. If a business is giving away something, we ask, "What's the catch? That's too good to be true."

God has provided us with every blessing we have. However, whatever reimbursement we attempt to make is so nominal that God has no need to take our payment. When we owe another person something, such as rent or car payments, one reason we must pay that debt is that the other person needs the money. Yet in God's case, He does not need anything from us. We need Him; He does not need us (Acts 17:25). His power, might, wisdom and glory can never be diminished by whatever we withhold from Him. His omnipotence, omniscience and omnipresence are not determined by the praise, adoration and worship that we offer to Him. He is the almighty God, whether we acknowledge it or not. He is not dependent on us; we are dependent on Him.

When we are convinced that we owe God nothing, we cannot leave it there. We will, of necessity, react to His goodness and grace. When we realize that God's blessings do not fall into the category of "too good to be true," what will our response be? When we comprehend the magnitude of what He has done, can we merely say about God's will, "That's just something God wants us to do; we can do it if we want to, and if we don't want to, we don't have to"?

How Shall We
Respond to God's Love?

When we really grasp the concept of owing nothing to God, then our relief and thankfulness and joy will be so great that we will respond to Him in love and gratitude. As we begin to see how much He loves us, we want to return that love. The response of a grateful heart will be to do everything we can to show God that we appreciate what He has done and that we love Him for it. We cannot ignore His gift.

Legalism or Love?

God loves us, and He has shown us how much He loves us by what He has given us and what He has done for us. If we really think about the significance of His gift to us, we will want to do everything we can to please Him, to show Him that we love Him, too. It will be the difference between "Aw, do I have to do what He says?" and "Oh, I want to do what will please Him!" This is the difference between the drudgery of duty because we owe obedience and the pleasure of pleasing God because we find delight in doing His will. It is the difference between legalism and love.

Let me illustrate. When I was a teenager, there was a certain young man whose attention I desired. One day I wore a blouse I thought was pretty, but by a casual comment he left the impression that it was a style he did not consider attractive. Consequently, I no longer enjoyed wearing that blouse. Why? Because I owed it to him to stop wearing it? Of course not. However, because of my love for him, I really did want to please him; if he did not like that blouse, neither did I. That happened more than 45 years ago, and I still find satisfaction in pleasing that same no-longer-so-young man.

That is the way it is when we want to please God by showing our love for Him. We want to spend our entire lives doing whatever will please Him, not us. Besides, He knows us better than we know ourselves, and what pleases Him is always what is best for us.

It is not sufficient to say to God, "Thank you, Lord, for saving me. Oh, yes – and I love you." We need to demonstrate that love. We must show God that we love Him. If a young man keeps phoning his girlfriend saying, "I love you, Honey," but never sees her, never spends time with her, never does anything that she wants to do, she may correctly decide that he really does not love her. He must demonstrate his love by his actions, or she will not believe him.

To Love Is to Obey

In John 14 Jesus Himself tells us how we can show our love: "If you love me, you will obey what I command" (v. 15). "Whoever has my commands and obeys them, he is the one who loves me" (v. 21). "If anyone loves me, he will obey my teaching" (v. 23). "He who does not love me will not obey my teaching" (v. 24).

Even Jesus demonstrated His love for God by obeying Him. In John 14:31 Jesus tells us: "[T]he world must learn that I love the Father and that I do exactly what my Father has commanded me." If Jesus loves the Father and obeys Him so completely, dare we do any less?

In obedience to God, Jesus provided the way for our salvation even though it meant tremendous suffering for Him. He expressed His great love both for the Father and for us by His actions on our behalf. If Jesus showed His love through His behavior toward others, should we not do the same?

First John emphasizes how important it is for us to love not only God but also other people:

> Dear friends, let us love one another, for love comes from God. ... This is love: ... that he ... sent his Son as an atoning sacrifice for our sins. ... [S]ince God so loved us, we also ought to love one another. (4:7, 10-11)

> We love because he first loved us. If anyone says, "I love God," yet hates his brother, he is a liar. For anyone who does not love his brother, whom he has seen, cannot love God, whom he has not seen. And he has given us this command: Whoever loves God must also love his brother. (4:19-21)

> Everyone ... who loves the father loves his child as well. This is how we know that we love the children of God: by loving God and carrying out his commands. This is love for God: to obey his commands. (5:1-3)

God's love for us, our love for God and our love for other human beings are all closely related. God's love for us is the basis of our love for others. Our love for God influences the way we treat everyone in our lives. We cannot claim to love God and then neglect our responsibilities toward one another.

It is obvious that obedience is the way to show God that we love Him. Therefore if we love God, we cannot say with my friend, "You can do it if you want to, and if you don't want to, you don't have to." If we love Him and know that He wants us to do a certain thing, we will choose to do it, whatever it is. The more we love Him the more earnestly we will obey Him.

We are free to choose to obey God; He does not force obedience and we do not owe it. Choosing to obey God is the most important decision we will ever make in our lives. The motivation for our obedience should be love and the desire to please God.

As stated before, the Cross does not drive us, it draws us to Christ. That is another way of saying that God does not force or demand anything from us. Although we owe Him nothing, He invites us, He wants us to do His will. First Timothy 2:4 tells us that God "wants all men to be saved and to come to a knowledge of the truth."

It is not solely a matter of keeping all the commands (legalism), but rather it is wanting to do what will please God (love). If the Scriptures give us an indication, even if it is not a command, that God prefers a certain thing or way of doing something, that should be enough for us. We will do it simply because we love Him and want to express that love to Him. We should not waste our time trying to figure out a way around what God has said. We certainly would not want to do anything that might displease Him.

Thus, if we love God, although we owe Him nothing, we will obey Him in everything.

The Obedient Life

God has high expectations for us, not because He is unreasonable but because He loves us so much. He is like devoted parents who want the very best for their children.

God wants us to want to obey Him, and He makes it as easy for us as He can. First John 5:3-5 assures us of this fact:

> This is love for God: to obey his commands. And his commands are not burdensome, for everyone born of God has overcome the world. This is the

victory that has overcome the world, even our faith. Who is it that overcomes the world? Only he who believes that Jesus is the Son of God.

Presuming that the Christian life is hard to live is the legalistic perspective. Assuming that God's commands are for our good is the perspective of those who obey out of love. Matthew 11:28-30 also tells us that God's way of life is not difficult:

> Come to me, all you who are weary and burdened, and I will give you rest. Take my yoke upon you and learn from me, for I am gentle and humble in heart, and you will find rest for your souls. For my yoke is easy and my burden is light.

Romans 12:1-2 tells us more about God's will:

> Therefore, I urge you, brothers, in view of God's mercy, to offer your bodies as living sacrifices, holy and pleasing to God – which is your spiritual worship. Do not conform any longer to the pattern of this world, but be transformed by the renewing of your mind. Then you will be able to test and approve what God's will is – his good, pleasing and perfect will.

That is another way of saying that God's way is the best way for us.

We should obey God, not because we owe it to Him, but because we are free to choose to obey Him and we want to return His love. When we make that choice, what kind of obedience does God want?

Little White Lies Are Okay, Right?

Some people think there are big sins and little sins; it is wrong to do big sins, but little ones, such as little white lies, are okay. We like to pick and choose what commands we want to obey, but that is not God's way. James 2:10-11 discusses the problem of keeping only part of God's laws:

> For whoever keeps the whole law and yet stumbles at just one point is guilty of breaking all of it.

For he who said, "Do not commit adultery," also
said, "Do not murder." If you do not commit adultery but do commit murder, you have become
a lawbreaker.

God's will is for us to obey all of His laws all of the time.
It is not our prerogative to choose which ones to obey. We
cannot say, "But we are free to do whatever we want!" First
Peter 2:16 responds to this attitude. "Live as free men, but
do not use your freedom as a cover-up for evil; live as servants of God."

Part of the problem is that we draw a line between right
and wrong, then we try to walk as close to that line as we can,
without stepping over onto the wrong side. Instead we should
walk as far away from that line as we can on the side that is
right. Stay where you know it is right, instead of staying where
you hope maybe it is okay.

A friend thought her visit to Africa would not be complete
without seeing a lion. Thus she was pleased to find one in a
cage in a park she toured. Because the lion was behind bars,
my friend thought that she could safely go near the cage to
get a better look. However, as she stood there, the lion reached
through the bars and mauled her leg. She learned the hard
way that she should not have ventured so close to that di-
viding line between safety and danger.

Can't We Just Almost Obey?

An example is found in 1 Samuel 15 of a person who tried
to obey God, but not completely. Samuel gave King Saul a message from God that included the command to "attack the
Amalekites and totally destroy everything that belongs to them.
Do not spare them; put to death men and women, children and
infants, cattle and sheep, camels and donkeys" (v. 3).

That message could not have been stated more clearly. Saul
mustered his forces and went to battle against the Amalekites
and their king, Agag. Although Saul and his army knew exactly what God wanted them to do, they had their own ideas
of what was right.

But Saul and the army spared Agag and the best of
the sheep and cattle, the fat calves and lambs –

everything that was good. These they were unwilling to destroy completely, but everything that was despised and weak they totally destroyed. (v. 9)

They obeyed only the part of the command that they wanted to obey.

God was not pleased.

God sent Samuel back to Saul with another message. When Samuel approached, Saul greeted him by saying, "I have carried out the Lord's instructions" (v. 13).

Samuel's response was to ask for the meaning of the animal sounds he heard. Saul had a ready response: "The soldiers brought them from the Amalekites; they spared the best of the sheep and cattle to sacrifice to the Lord your God, but we totally destroyed the rest" (v. 15).

Samuel then gave Saul the message from the Lord, repeating what Saul had been told before the battle, and asking the question, "Why did you not obey the Lord?" (v. 19).

Surely Saul had the intelligence to understand the message from God, but his answer is amazing:

"But I did obey the Lord," Saul said. "I went on the mission the Lord assigned me. I completely destroyed the Amalekites and brought back Agag their king. The soldiers took sheep and cattle from the plunder, the best of what was devoted to God, in order to sacrifice them to the Lord your God at Gilgal." (vv. 20-21)

Saul knew exactly what God wanted, but he and his soldiers thought they had a better idea. They would give these things to God as offerings instead of dealing with them in the way God had commanded.

God was not pleased.

Samuel finally convinced Saul of his error when he said, "To obey is better than sacrifice ... Because you have rejected the word of the Lord, he has rejected you as king" (vv. 22-23).

Saul finally admitted, "I have sinned. I violated the Lord's command and your instructions. I was afraid of the people and so I gave in to them" (v. 24).

Saul's problem was that he thought he obeyed God "close enough." However, God is not satisfied with anything less than exact, total obedience. Partial commitment is really no commitment at all. To God, complete obedience is much better than any sacrifice.

It is a sobering thought that while Saul's lack of obedience merely cost him his earthly kingdom, our lack of obedience can cost us the eternal kingdom.

God Wants Total Obedience

As you read through the Bible, notice the frequency of such statements as: he "did everything just as God commanded" (Genesis 6:22); "obeyed me and kept my requirements, my commands, my decrees and my laws" (26:5); "listen carefully" (Exodus 15:26; 23:22); "obey me fully" (19:5); "do everything" (19:8); "do all that I say" (23:22); "make [it] exactly like the pattern I will show you" (25:9); "just as the Lord commanded" (36:1; 39:32, 42-43; 40:16-32); "careful to obey" (Leviticus 26:3); "must do exactly" (Numbers 15:14); "do not add [or] subtract but keep [his] commands" (Deuteronomy 4:2); "be sure to follow" (5:1); "do not turn aside to the right or to the left" (v. 32); "if we are careful to obey all ... that will be our righteousness" (6:25). There are many more examples; these are only a few references from the beginning of the Old Testament.

Nowhere in the Bible does God say, "It's okay if you don't want to obey everything. Just do the best you think you can, and I'll settle for whatever makes you feel comfortable."

Psalm 119 honors the word of God. Each stanza of that psalm praises God's word. In almost every stanza there is included the idea of the importance of obedience. Obeying the word of God is the way we honor and give reverence to His word.

One might say "Aha! But that's all from the Old Testament! Today we follow the New Testament!" We know, however, that God does not change – He is the same yesterday, today and forever (Malachi 3:6; Hebrews 13:8). God lays down principles with some specifics. Some details of what we should do have changed, but the broad principles remain the same. The Old Testament is given to teach us, to be an example to lead us to a better understanding of God (1 Corinthians 10:6).

Hebrews 2:2-3 shows us that we today must obey God's laws as surely as those who lived under His old law. "For if the message spoken by angels was binding, and every violation and disobedience received its just punishment, how shall we escape if we ignore such a great salvation?"

The Great Commission in Matthew 28:18-20 emphasizes the necessity of total obedience:

> Then Jesus came to them and said, "All authority in heaven and on earth has been given to me. Therefore go and make disciples of all nations, baptizing them in the name of the Father and of the Son and of the Holy Spirit, and teaching them to obey everything I have commanded you. And surely I will be with you always, to the very end of the age."

Belief, or faith, and obedience are closely linked in several passages, as are unbelief and disobedience. The more faith we have, the more completely and precisely we are willing to obey. Israel was often in trouble because "everyone did as he saw fit" (Judges 17:6; 21:25). In other words, they chose what, and if, they wanted to obey. They lacked the faith to do things God's way. The lack of enough faith to make us obey completely is also a problem today. We, too, want to obey only those laws we like.

If we do not have enough faith in God, we will not obey Him.

> See to it, brothers, that none of you has a sinful, unbelieving heart that turns away from the living God. But encourage one another daily, as long as it is called Today, so that none of you may be hardened by sin's deceitfulness. We have come to share in Christ if we hold firmly till the end the confidence we had at first. (Hebrews 3:12-14)

The connection between obedience and faith is plainly stated in Romans 1:5: "Through him and for his name's sake, we received grace and apostleship to call people from among all the Gentiles to the obedience that comes from faith." Our obedience is dependent upon our faith.

When we do not obey, we sin. First John 3:4-6 explains more about sin:

Everyone who sins breaks the law; in fact, sin is law-lessness. But you know that he appeared so that he might take away our sins. And in him is no sin. No one who lives in him keeps on sinning. No one who continues to sin has either seen him or known him.

This verse does not say we can do no wrong. It means rather that when we choose to obey, we want to do what is right, and we try to obey. We must turn our backs on sin and turn our faces toward God – that is the direction we want to be heading. We need to keep His holiness and His perfect way in front of us as our goal, as something to aim for as we try to live worthy lives. When we decide that we want to obey God, that automatically takes care of many other decisions. If we see from our studies of the Bible that a certain thing would please God, then without further question we will want to do it and we will obey. We do not have to decide if we will obey this time.

Maturing in the Lord

Paul makes an important point in Philippians 3:12-16:

Not that I have already obtained all this, or have already been made perfect, but I press on to take hold of that for which Christ Jesus took hold of me. Brothers, I do not consider myself yet to have taken hold of it. But one thing I do: Forgetting what is behind and straining toward what is ahead, I press on toward the goal to win the prize for which God has called me heavenward in Christ Jesus. All of us who are mature should take such a view of things. And if on some point you think differently, that too God will make clear to you. Only let us live up to what we have already attained.

God is never satisfied with less than our best. We must obey Him to the very best of our abilities in everything. We should continue to try to reach the goal of heaven. God is calling us to Him, but we have to do our part.

Living a worthy life will mean different things at different stages of our lives. Activities appropriate for a 2-year-old may not be appropriate for a 10-year-old. Thus a mature Christian is capable of a higher level of performance. We must always live up to our capabilities. As we grow in Christ, more is expected of us.

Those of us who have been in Christ for many years should keep this principle in mind. We must remember that new Christians are babes in Christ. We should not immediately expect from them the same level of maturity that has taken us years to attain. They need our patience, even as we need patience from those who are more mature than we.

God has not specified everything in black and white, so there will be judgment calls. We need to know the principles involved so that we can make mature choices. We need to continue to learn God's will so that we can grow in the ability to obey Him completely.

A word of caution is in order here. If you have really grasped the concept of not owing God anything, then do not be upset when someone says we must do certain things, as long as these things are in agreement with biblical teaching. It is not contradictory to say that we owe God nothing but that He has given commands that we must obey if we want to please Him. We cannot say, "Oh, I don't owe God anything, so I can do whatever I want; it doesn't matter!" It does matter to each soul's salvation. We can never do anything, even total, complete obedience, to earn the right to go to heaven. Yet because we are each held accountable for our own actions, our disobedience can prevent our going to heaven (Ezekiel 18:4; Romans 6:23).

The Bible tells us certain things that God requires of us or that is our duty to do. An example is in Micah 6:8: "And what does the Lord require of you? To act justly and to love mercy and to walk humbly with your God."

Another example is in Ecclesiastes 12:13: "Fear God and keep his commandments, for this is the whole duty of man."

Romans 6:1-2 is emphatic that it is important for us to turn from sin. "What shall we say, then? Shall we go on sinning so that grace may increase? By no means! We died to sin; how can we live in it any longer?" As we mature in the Lord we realize more and more the necessity of total obedience to God.

Is This Legalism?

Complete, total, precise obedience is not necessarily legalism. Legalism is when someone says, "You owe it to God to do this, this, and this. You must do it because it is required of you – you have to do it; you must go through these motions." We are talking instead about joyfully choosing to show our love to God by pleasing Him. We are talking about obedience and service from the heart, not from external pressures.

Jesus condemned the Pharisees for their legalism in Matthew 23. They required the Jews to obey the many rules they had made. In verse 23, Jesus says:

> Woe to you, teachers of the law and Pharisees, you hypocrites! You give a tenth of your spices – mint, dill and cumin. But you have neglected the more important matters of the law – justice, mercy and faithfulness. You should have practiced the latter, without neglecting the former.

Jesus did not condemn them for being careful to obey the laws concerning the smallest details, laws that required them to tithe even the herbs that grew in their kitchen gardens. He said it was right for them to do that. Their problem was that they did not obey all God's laws as scrupulously as they did a few chosen ones. They neglected obedience to the great principles governing human conduct before God. God is not pleased with obedience to only some of His commands.

What If I Cannot Obey Everything?

The moment we come out of the baptismal waters we are forgiven and thus pure, but being human, we do not stay that way. We must realize that we are not perfect – there will be times when we do not do what we know we should, or when we do what we know we should not. We want to do what is right, but sometimes we fail. Paul stated the same problem in Romans 7:15: "I do not understand what I do. For what I want to do I do not do, but what I hate I do."

When we fail to obey everything precisely, have we lost our chance, and do we have to return the gift God gave us? No!

Imagine a toddler, just learning to walk, and his adoring daddy. Daddy is holding out his arms encouraging the baby to take steps toward him. The baby wants to walk, and the daddy encourages, "Come on! You can do it! Come on – I'll help you! I love you so much – come to me!" The baby, smiling with excitement, takes two or three faltering steps toward Daddy's outstretched arms, but stumbles and falls down. Can you imagine that doting daddy harshly saying, "Now you've done it! You fell! You're no child of mine if you can't walk by yourself! You had your chance and you blew it! Now get out of here!" No, that loving daddy is going to reach out quickly, take hold of that toddler's hand, and help him learn to walk properly. It may take a thousand tumbles before the child learns to walk, but the daddy is still there, still helping.

That is the kind of loving, forgiving Father we have in heaven. The prophet Isaiah describes the tenderness of the care God gives us:

> He tends his flock like a shepherd:
> He gathers the lambs in his arms
> and carries them close to his heart;
>   he gently leads those that have young. (40:11)

> For this is what the Lord says: ...
> "As a mother comforts her child,
>   so will I comfort you." (66:12-13)

The Beauty of Holiness

When we realize the kind of heavenly Father we have, our lives will be happier, more joyful, fuller, richer and more fulfilling. There is nothing so beautiful as living life the way God intends for us to live it. Everything we do must fit into the framework of a worthy life. The more we know about God from His word, the more we trust Him; the more we see His marvelous gifts of grace to us, the more we will love Him. The more we trust and love Him, the more we will obey Him in everything.

Our lives will never be what God wants them to be unless we are totally, completely and joyfully committed to obeying Him from the heart. Only then will we be truly free to live worthy lives in His service. It is not enough that we go through the motions of obedience. We must have the attitude of obedience; that is, we must cultivate the attitude that we shall willingly obey anything and everything God wants. This must not be a blind, unthinking obedience, but rather an obedience that joins us with God as we try to have the mind of Christ and be one with Him. Obedience must become a part of our inner being; in our very nature we must become obedient. Then we will faithfully do the right thing even on those occasions when we may not feel like it.

Our salvation is a gift from God – a free gift of grace. Thus we are no longer debtors; we have been totally forgiven and we actually owe God nothing. However, when we realize what Christ did for us in His death and how much He loves us, our natural response will be to want to return that love. In John 14:15 Christ told us exactly how to do so: "If you love me, you will obey what I command." If we really love Him, we will be totally committed to doing everything He wants. We will gladly obey Him completely because of the love we have for Him.

Although we owe Him nothing, we will obey Him in everything.

Discussion Questions

1. What does "choosing to serve God" mean to you? How does that choice affect your everyday decisions?
2. How is your attitude toward God influenced by the statement, "The Cross draws us to Christ; it does not drive us"? How do you respond when you know there is something that God wants you to do, even if you do not see it as a direct command?
3. In what ways is it difficult to understand and accept the concept that God has completely canceled our debt to Him? How can you say that you owe God nothing? Are there things that you do owe Him?
4. Think about some time in your life when you were forgiven by a friend for some wrong you did. How did you feel? How did you react? Compare this experience with being forgiven by God for all your sins.
5. How would you explain to a non-Christian that God considers Christians to be blameless even though we have sinned?

6. List some ways in which God has shown His tremendous love for you personally. What specific things can you do to show Him that you want to return that love?

7. Compare Saul's actions recorded in 1 Samuel 15 with some time in your life when you "nearly" obeyed God. Why is complete obedience necessary to please God? Why should you have to do everything He says?

8. What connections have you seen in your own life between faith and obedience?

9. What is your definition of "legalism"? How can you avoid being legalistic in your life while still trying to give total obedience to God?

10. You will not always obey perfectly and completely. What is God's reaction when you do something you should not? What hope is left for you when you sin after Christ bought you and set you free?

11. In the early fifth century, Augustine wrote, "Love God and do as you please." What do you think about this statement? In what ways is it true? In what ways is it false?

12. What parallels do you see between the situation described in Judges 17:6; 21:25 when "everyone did what was right in his own eyes" and the situation in our world today? What can you do to make things better?

CHAPTER 3

That Awe-Full Feeling

*"The fear of the Lord is a fountain of life,
turning a man from the snares of death" (Proverbs 14:27).*

Have you ever felt deep within yourself the surging power of a mighty storm as huge trees whipped almost to the earth before the raging wind? Have you wondered in amazement how this could happen, but perceived that the power of the storm is nothing compared with the power of God?

Have you ever stood alone beneath a spectacular array of stars on a dark, clear night, feeling so small beside the enormity and beauty of the universe, yet sensing the nearness of God?

Have you ever been bewildered by the instinct of a flock of geese migrating in V formation, all the while knowing that the infinite wisdom of God has planned their actions for them?

Have you ever gazed into the eyes of a newborn baby and marveled at the miracle of God's creation of life?

If you have, then you have encountered that awe-full feeling.

Usually we think of the word "awful" as meaning only something horrible, appalling or terrible. However, it can also refer to something that is deeply impressive or reverential, something that is awe-inspiring.

Using the spelling "awe-full" emphasizes being filled with awe, reverence and even fear in the presence of the Almighty

God, the Creator, the Savior, the Lord of all, who alone has all wisdom and power and glory.

Although it is awe-inspiring to think of the beauties and wonders of nature that God has provided for us, it is even more awesome to think about the marvelous gifts of a spiritual nature He has given us. We cannot understand how or why He loves us and cares for us, but He does. As we try to comprehend His blessings, deep feelings will be stirred within us – such as joy, gratitude, love, thankfulness, peacefulness and amazement.

Awe, reverence and fear of God should have a prominent position among these reactions. Yet awe is something that is often overlooked, perhaps because we do not understand it. Maybe we are even a little embarrassed by reverence. We think that fearing the Lord was something done by past generations that we no longer need to do. However, if we understand what the Bible means by these words, we will see that we need awe, reverence and fear of God today as much as ever.

What Is Awe?

Webster's Dictionary defines "awe" as "great fear, dread, terror; the reverential fear felt for the Divine Being; emotion inspired by something dreadful and sublime; solemn wonder, profound reverence."

"Reverence" means "honor or respect because of position or relationship, deference; profound respect mingled with fear and affection, veneration."

It is difficult to define any one of these words (awe, reverence and fear of God) without making reference to the others. They are such closely related responses to the power and wisdom of God that they cannot be completely separated. However, a few explanatory comments may help illuminate some aspects of their meanings.

Awe is the wonder that fills us when we encounter the marvels of nature. We wonder how bumblebees fly, how butterflies migrate, or how the colors of the rainbow or a sunset can be so breathtakingly beautiful that we yearn to see them again. Reverence is acknowledging that God alone has the power and wisdom to create these awe-inspiring wonders of nature.

Awe is the perception of a power we cannot control. It is knowing that we are in the presence of One who is greater, better and mightier than we are. Reverence is our attitude toward God because of that knowledge. It is recognizing the holiness of God, becoming aware of His supreme majesty and then acting appropriately.

To fear God is to know that punishment is promised to those who rebel against Him. It is wanting to conduct ourselves properly in order to avoid that punishment. To fear God is to appreciate our place in His scheme of things. It is to know that His love for us is beyond understanding – we neither earn nor deserve His love, yet He freely gives it to us.

When we realize we are in the loving care of the almighty God, the awe we sense makes us want to be better than we have ever been before. It inspires in us feelings of both insignificance and uplift.

Awe, reverence and fear of God are all necessary for acceptable worship. Among our responses are feelings of fascination, devotion, adoration, worship and trust. We also feel a certain amount of fear and, yes, even dread and anxiety.

Attributes of God

Focusing on the attributes of God will help us understand and experience that awe-full feeling. The following traits do not describe God fully, but they are especially relevant to our study.

God is:

Omnipotent. He is all-powerful, with unlimited authority and infinite capacity.

Omnipresent. He is present in all places at all times.

Omniscient. He is all-wise and all-knowing. He has infinite awareness, understanding and insight. He possesses universal and complete knowledge.

Omnificent. He is unlimited in creative power, creating all that comes into existence.

Omni-loving. Although this attribute may not be in the dictionary, it is accurately descriptive because God Himself is love. How infinite, all-encompassing, unconditional and awe-inspiring is His love for us!

As we meditate on these aspects of God, our hearts will be filled with awe. As we realize the enormity of His power and love, we will fear Him. Does that mean that we will be afraid and frightened of Him, or does it mean that we will respect, reverence and honor Him?

Fear of God

Some people find it difficult to accept a God who punishes severely. Yet others are drawn to a God who deals justly with those who deserve punishment. Some people say that it is wrong to fear God – to be terrified of anyone or anything. Others contend that it is good for us to fear God – to know what He is capable of doing and to respect Him for it. Obviously there are great differences in the understanding of the "fear of God." What does the Bible say about fearing God?

Many scriptures emphasize both the blessings that come from fearing God and the importance of fearing Him. Fear of God, according to the Bible, is a positive thing. It is something that we need to have, something that is good for us. Some examples will help us understand this.

God loves all His creatures just as a parent loves his children. That love is expressed in a special way toward those who fear Him. This truth is stated in several verses of Psalm 103:

> For as high as the heavens are above the earth,
>   so great is his love for those who fear him. (v. 11)

> As a father has compassion on his children,
>   so the Lord has compassion on those who fear
>   him. (v. 13)

> But from everlasting to everlasting
>   the Lord's love is with those who fear him,
>   and his righteousness with their children's
>   children –
> with those who keep his covenant
>   and remember to obey his precepts. (vv. 17-18)

These verses indicate that fearing God should not be frightening but instead is something to be desired for its benefits.

God's love is especially abundant for those who fear Him, and we show our fear through faithful obedience to Him. After the Israelites received the Ten Commandments, they agreed to listen to God's words and obey Him. In Deuteronomy 5:29 God spoke as a loving parent who wants what is best for His children. "Oh, that their hearts would be inclined to fear me and keep all my commands always, so that it might go well with them and their children forever!"

Sometimes we may feel that God wants too much from us, but we must realize that everything He asks of us, including His command to fear Him, is really for our own good. This truth is expressed clearly in Deuteronomy 10:12-13:

> And now, O Israel, what does the Lord your God ask of you but to fear the Lord your God, to walk in all his ways, to love him, to serve the Lord your God with all your heart and with all your soul, and to observe the Lord's commands and decrees that I am giving you today for your own good?

Even the name of God is awe-inspiring because of His holiness. After telling of some of the mighty works of God, Psalm 111:9 states that "holy and awesome is his name." Verse 10 continues with the importance of fearing and obeying God in order to have wisdom and understanding:

> The fear of the Lord is the beginning of wisdom;
> all who follow his precepts have good understanding.
> To him belongs eternal praise.

Awe and respect for God give an insight into reality denied to those without reverence for Him. It is notable that all these verses connect fearing God with obeying Him and following His instructions.

God spoke the heavens and the earth into existence. How can we possibly ignore such mighty power as is shown in Psalm 33:6-9:

> The word of the Lord created the heavens;

all the host of heaven was formed at
   his command.
He gathered into a heap the waters
   of the sea,
he laid up the deeps in his store-
   chambers.
Let the whole world fear the Lord
   and all earth's inhabitants stand in
     awe of him.
For he spoke, and it was;
   he commanded, and there it stood." (REB)

When we learn to fear the Lord, we also learn to trust Him
– to rely on Him and to believe that He is our best help in any
kind of trouble or problem. He helps all who fear Him, not
just those people we might consider important. Psalm 115
tells us of this blessing:

You who fear him, trust in the Lord –
   he is their help and shield. (v. 11)
he will bless those who fear the Lord –
   small and great alike. (v. 13)

Another aspect of the fear of the Lord is identified in
Proverbs 8:13. Wisdom personified speaks:

To fear the Lord is to hate evil;
   I hate pride and arrogance,
   evil behavior and perverse speech.

Fear of the Lord must go hand-in-hand with hatred of evil.
A good gardener is aware that to have a beautiful garden it
is not enough merely to love flowers, one must also hate the
weeds. We can never hope to be wise and understanding until we learn to fear God enough to root sin out of our lives.

Benefits of fearing the Lord as well as problems of those
who do not fear Him are discussed in Proverbs 14:

He whose walk is upright fears the Lord,
   but he whose ways are devious despises
     him. (v. 2)
A wise man fears the Lord and shuns evil,
   but a fool is hotheaded and reckless. (v. 16)

> He who fears the Lord has a secure fortress,
>   and for his children it will be a refuge.
> The fear of the Lord is a fountain of life,
>   turning a man from the snares of death.
>   (vv. 26-27)

God can reward us, but He can also punish us. The whole duty of man is summed up in the admonition to fear God. Fearing God has a deeper and more constructive meaning than being frightened or terrified of Him. It includes obeying all of God's will for us.

> Now all has been heard;
>   here is the conclusion of the matter:
> Fear God and keep his commandments,
>   for this is the whole duty of man.
>   (Ecclesiastes 12:13)

Matthew 10:28 shows that fear of the Lord also includes the idea of being frightened of what He can do. "Do not be afraid of those who kill the body but cannot kill the soul. Rather, be afraid of the one who can destroy both soul and body in hell."

According to Hebrews 12:28-29, acceptable worship to God includes proper reverence and awe. "Therefore, since we are receiving a kingdom that cannot be shaken, let us be thankful, and so worship God acceptably with reverence and awe, for our God is a consuming fire." We do not approach this kind of fire casually. Instead, we treat it with great respect.

Everyone must fear God, not only on this earth but also in heaven. Revelation 14:6-7 points out the universality of the gospel and the need to fear and worship God:

> Then I saw another angel flying in midair, and he had the eternal gospel to proclaim to those who live on the earth – to every nation, tribe, language and people. He said in a loud voice, "Fear God and give him glory, because the hour of his judgment has come. Worship him who made the heavens, the earth, the sea and the springs of water."

Fear at Mount Sinai

One aspect of fearing God is being terrified at what His mighty power is capable of doing to us if we disobey Him, even unwittingly. This meaning is obvious in the scene at Mount Sinai when God gave the Law to Moses in Exodus 19 and 20. First, God told Moses to remind the people of His overwhelming power exhibited in leading them out of Egypt. Then, He explained what would happen next. He was going to come in a dense cloud, and the people would hear Him speaking with Moses.

Exodus 19:10-13 continues the narrative:

> And the Lord said to Moses, "Go to the people and consecrate them today and tomorrow. Have them wash their clothes and be ready by the third day, because on that day the Lord will come down on Mount Sinai in the sight of all the people. Put limits for the people around the mountain and tell them, `Be careful that you do not go up the mountain or touch the foot of it. Whoever touches the mountain shall surely be put to death. ... Whether man or animal, he shall not be permitted to live.' Only when the ram's horn sounds a long blast may they go up to the mountain."

The people had good reason to be afraid of what would happen if they disobeyed. They knew from experience that God would keep His word. Therefore Moses and the people made the required preparations.

Exodus 19:16, 18-19 tells us what happened next:

> On the morning of the third day there was thunder and lightning, with a thick cloud over the mountain, and a very loud trumpet blast. Everyone in the camp trembled. ... [T]he whole mountain trembled violently, and the sound of the trumpet grew louder and louder. Then Moses spoke and the voice of God answered him.

Try to imagine yourself at Sinai with the Israelites. Can you feel the awe and reverence they must have felt? This meeting with God was so important that it was necessary for the people to prepare themselves. It was truly awe-inspiring to come into the presence of God Himself. Sometimes we do not feel the magnitude and significance of the privilege of coming into God's presence. Dare we approach His presence either carelessly or disrespectfully? There was nothing flippant nor disinterested about the attitude of the people of Israel on this occasion.

> When the people saw the thunder and lightning and heard the trumpet and saw the mountain in smoke, they trembled with fear. They stayed at a distance and said to Moses, "Speak to us yourself and we will listen. But do not have God speak to us or we will die."
>
> Moses said to the people, "Do not be afraid. God has come to test you, so that the fear of God will be with you to keep you from sinning." (20:18-20)

Moses made it very clear that, although the people were terrified of what God could do, they should not be paralyzed by that terror, nor should we. Incapacitating fear has no place in the lives of God's people. We should not be afraid of God, but we should fear him. Awe and reverence include the fear that we might displease God. Reverential trust will make us want to please and obey Him.

There is value in fear as a preventative. Fearing God will help each of us to live the kind of worthy life to which He has called us.

In Hebrews 12:18-29 the writer makes an application for people today of this scene at Mount Sinai:

> You have not come to a mountain that can be touched and that is burning with fire; to darkness, gloom and storm; to a trumpet blast or to such a voice speaking words, so that those who heard it begged that no further word be spoken to them, because they could not bear what was commanded: "If even an animal touches the mountain, it must be stoned." The sight was so terrifying that Moses said, "I am trembling with fear."

But you have come to Mount Zion, to the heavenly Jerusalem, the city of the living God. You have come to thousands upon thousands of angels in joyful assembly, to the church of the firstborn, whose names are written in heaven. You have come to God, the judge of all men, to the spirits of righteous men made perfect, to Jesus the mediator of a new covenant, and to the sprinkled blood that speaks a better word than the blood of Abel.

See to it that you do not refuse him who speaks. If they did not escape when they refused him who warned them on earth, how much less will we, if we turn away from him who warns us from heaven? At that time his voice shook the earth, but now he has promised, "Once more will I shake not only the earth but also the heavens." The words "once more" indicate the removing of what can be shaken – that is, created things – so that what cannot be shaken may remain.

Therefore, since we are receiving a kingdom that cannot be shaken, let us be thankful, and so worship God acceptably with reverence and awe, for our God is a consuming fire.

The conclusion drawn by the writer of Hebrews is that we should worship God acceptably with reverence and awe. If we have proper reverence and awe before God, our worship will not be thoughtless or careless. It is not acceptable to claim to be worshiping God when we are not even thinking about Him – when we allow our minds to roam far afield during periods of apparent worship. Neither is it acceptable when our worship is directed by its entertainment value to us, rather than being centered on God and His holiness.

Although the giving of the law on Mount Sinai was a unique situation, we still should recognize, as did the ancient Israelites, that coming into the presence of God requires some preparation. It is true that God is with his people at all times, but there is a special time when we approach him in worship as a community. We cannot expect to please God if we are careless in our attitude toward worshiping him.

Preparation for Worship

We might compare planning and preparing by the leaders for an assembly of the church with planning and preparing a dinner. When friends are invited for dinner, the gracious host and hostess want to make the guests feel at home. Thus they spend time and thought in deciding on the menu, acquiring and preparing the food, creating a pleasant atmosphere, setting the table attractively, and making everything as appealing as possible, all the while considering the likes and dislikes of their guests. Such prearrangements say to the guests: "You are important to us. We care enough about you to spend the time and thought necessary to make adequate preparations to be sure that you are pleased. We are happy to have you here, and we really want you to enjoy this occasion."

Spontaneous worship might be compared to having unexpected company for dinner. When we willingly prepare dinner for that last-minute guest, our actions say: "We are glad you are here even if the dinner has not been planned. Let's make the best of the moment and enjoy each other's company. It is being together that counts, not what we have to eat."

There is room for both types of events in our lives. We are enriched by each situation. However, if we invite someone to dinner at a specified time and then wait until that time arrives to begin thinking about what we are going to serve, that will send a different message to the guest. Our lack of planning and preparation will say: "You really are not very important to us. We did not choose to spend any time or thought in preparation for you, but since you are here, we'll do something and maybe it will be okay."

In all three of these illustrations, God represents the guest at the dinner. When we worship Him, His likes and dislikes must be considered first, not ours. He is the one to be honored by what we do.

We need to recognize the importance of God's presence and act accordingly. When we see a beautiful sunset, we may be overwhelmed with joy and gratitude. As we feel His nearness, prayers of praise and thanksgiving well up within us to glorify God for His creation. Such spontaneous worship is certainly appropriate and pleasing to God. However, when we know that we are going to assemble with other Christians at a certain time and place, is it not reasonable to think that the occasion is important enough for planning and preparation to take place? If we are willing to spend time and thought to make a dinner in our homes pleasing to a guest, how much more should we plan the spiritual feast when we know that God will be with us there!

Although God is always with each of us individually, it is a special time when we come together as a church to meet with God and He with us. It is a time that is important to our well-being as the family of God.

Will the holy respect that we feel for God make any difference in the way we worship Him? The answer should be a resounding "Yes!"

How would you react if you were invited to a meeting with the most esteemed and influential person on this earth? Would you be late? Would you insist that the meeting be conducted according to your wishes? Would you wear the same thing you might wear to a picnic? Would you perhaps decide that person was not important enough for you even to make the effort to attend? Or would you have a more respectful attitude?

It is not enough that the leaders of the congregation make adequate preparations for the activities in the assembly of the church. It is just as important that all of us prepare ourselves to worship God in a worthy manner. The Israelites at Sinai spent three days consecrating themselves, washing their clothes and making other preparations. So, too, should we recognize the importance of meeting together as a community with God and preparing for it.

The assembly of the church should not be a fashion show or merely a social occasion. Yet we should spend adequate time being certain we are appropriately clothed and clean, both physically and spiritually, before we come into God's presence. The best preparation for the regular assemblies of the church is the time spent daily in Bible study, prayer, meditation and deeds of love performed for others.

If we feel that coming into the Lord's presence is really not very important (or if we exhibit that attitude by our actions), then we are showing inadequate respect for Him and all that

He has done for us. However, if coming before the Lord with fellow Christians is important to us, we will make the necessary effort to arrive on time for every assembly of the church. We will not be occupied with our own leisure activities right up to the last moment so that we have no time to prepare our minds and bodies for this important meeting. If we prepare for worship by meditating on the glory and power of God, we will contemplate the meaning of the words as we sing praises to Him. Our hearts and minds will be centered on the adoration we are offering the almighty God. We will not center our minds on what someone else is wearing or how the child in front of us is misbehaving.

If we do not show reverence and awe when we are in the assembly of the church before God, we probably will not show reverence and awe at other times in our lives. When we come into God's presence in that special way, we are more likely than at any other time to acknowledge His presence.

In Nehemiah 8:5-6 we see one way the people of God showed their respect:

> Ezra opened the book. ... And as he opened it, the people all stood up. Ezra praised the Lord, the great God; and all the people lifted their hands and responded, "Amen! Amen!" Then they bowed down and worshiped the Lord with their faces to the ground.

As they were assembled together, they stood to listen to the word of God as a sign of respect. Then they bowed and worshiped in humility. Standing may not be recognized today as a sign of respect, but if we are awed by the mighty power of God, we will find ways of adequately showing our respect for him.

Balancing Fear with Love

Fear of God should be a significant part of our worship to Him. However we should not emphasize fear so much that we lose sight of the fact that we are free to choose willingly and gladly to serve God and thus please Him. Love is an essential balancing factor, as we see from 1 John 4:13-18:

> We know that we live in him and he in us, because
> he has given us of his Spirit. And we have seen and
> testify that the Father has sent his Son to be the Savior
> of the world. If anyone acknowledges that Jesus is
> the Son of God, God lives in him and he in God. And
> so we know and rely on the love God has for us.
>   God is love. Whoever lives in love lives in God,
> and God in him. Love is made complete among us
> so that we will have confidence on the day of judg-
> ment, because in this world we are like him. There
> is no fear in love. But perfect love drives out fear,
> because fear has to do with punishment. The man
> who fears is not made perfect in love.

Fear, in the sense of being afraid of God, is appropriate at a certain stage of our spiritual development. Indeed it should remain operative at some level all through our lives; that is, we should always remember that we must obey God and that He can and will punish sin. As new Christians we may be frightened of God and His power to impose punishment on us for wrongdoing, but as we feel His love and learn to rely on Him, we respond to that love by becoming less fearful. As we grow in spiritual maturity, love emerges as the control-ling motive for our conduct. It is a love that is built on top of the fear of His mighty power. Reverence and awe for God are not lost; they are intensified by the marvel that such an all-knowing, all-powerful God can love us so profoundly.

God is a caring, tender Father who loves us more than we can imagine and who wants only what is best for us. He is our best friend, our confidant. We can approach His throne of grace with boldness, because part of the free gift of salva-tion is that we are His dearly beloved children. Ephesians 3:12 tells us: "In him and through faith in him we may approach God with freedom and confidence."

A high school English student wrote the following theme that illustrates very nicely that balance between fear and bold-ness that we should have when we approach God.

A VISION OF GLORY
by Ann Doyle
(Used by permission)

As I knelt beside my bed the other day, I saw something I had never really seen before: all at once I imagined myself in a giant hall.

The floors were of marble – porphyry and serpentine. There were long rows of travertine columns so tall that I could barely see the tops. But of course, I hardly dared look up. The hall was not especially wide – not more than 150-200 feet. I could easily see the rich tapestries which hung all along the walls. They were beautiful – heavenly. There was a bright light shining from the far end of the hall. It was very intense, but it was not harsh. I knew very well where it originated and to me it had always been a friendly light. There was a golden throne at the end of the hall and on it sat the greatest monarch the world has ever known. I trembled in his presence, and I shall never know what steadied my knees as I obeyed his command to come to him. Yes, I fear that gentle man with the friendly face! Those who do not fear him are those who have never met him. Yes, he is my father and I am his heir. Have you never feared your father?

I have been in that magnificent hall many times before and have spent many hours in the presence of this awesome monarch, but each visit is as frightening – and as pleasant – as the first. I shall never forget that first visit. I had been lost and hungry and the night was so cold, and dark, and long. After noticing a distant light, I began climbing toward it. The light came from the great hall. I was exhausted when I finally reached it.

There the king himself stretched out his hand to me and said, "Don't cry, my child. I will take care of you." And he did, too!

Almost every time I have approached the great throne I have recalled the first time I did so. Now I could also think of many other times I had approached it for many different reasons. It was a familiar place to me now. I had friends here and I greeted many of them along the way. In another time or place I would have been laughing with some of them in moments, but my business on this occasion was solemn. I had to report to the king on my progress as his ambassador, and I knew that I had not done well. Away from his presence I easily forgot my mission. I had become involved in many good but relatively unimportant pursuits and had failed to accomplish what I had been sent to do. Here, in the great hall, any reasons I might have given elsewhere to explain my failure were insignificant and impossible to justify. It was even difficult to understand how they could be considered excuses. They were all pointless. I could not even apologize, but only confessed my failure.

I expected the great king to be angry. I had known his anger before, yet somehow I think I would rather be thrown out of the hall than to hear my father say, "You have disappointed me." This is what his eyes said to me this time, but he did not dwell on it. He invited me to sit with him and we spoke in private for a long time. He spoke in those low, loving tones that only a father uses. He reminded me of all the things I had accomplished for him in the past, and I soon realized that it was really he who had accomplished these things because it was only when I knew what he wanted and obeyed it that I could see success. As I talked with my friend, I began to see things more clearly than before, and soon I was ready to return to my work. I knew once again what I must do and had a better idea how to do it.

After the more serious conversation was over, we visited for a long time. We talked of a thousand different things, for my boss is also my best friend.

When I finally left, I was not alone. A part of my father went with me and the atmosphere of the great hall surrounded us. The fear and the joy I had encountered here would give me my father's strength – strength to conquer the world, one day at a time.

Being in the presence of God is very serious and awe-inspiring. That does not mean, as some may think, that we must always go about with a solemn, sanctimonious face, never having any fun. God wants us to enjoy life. He wants what is best for us, and that includes all aspects of our lives. If we find that we cannot have "fun" while being aware of the presence of God, then we are having the wrong kind of "fun" and should find a lifestyle more in keeping with God's will. Only then will we find the true happiness and contentment that comes with fearing God.

What Produces Awe?

Recently I was privileged to accompany a college student on his first visit to Canterbury Cathedral in England. His awe was obvious as he walked around in amazement, marveling at the beautiful Gothic workmanship. His feelings of awe were inspired by what human craftsmen had done. If we can be awed by items made by mere humans, how much more should we stand in awe of the majestic handiwork of God!

We are surrounded by so many wonders that we often become oblivious to them. We take them for granted. Think of the loveliness of freshly opened flowers on a glorious spring morning, or the breathtaking colors of the fall landscape. We marvel at these and we make a point of experiencing them because there are only certain times that we can enjoy these awe-inspiring sights.

How long has it been since you allowed yourself to absorb the beauty of the stars? We take them for granted because they are there every night; even if the clouds obscure them, they are still there. However, if the stars came out in their glory only one night every 25 years, most of us would spend that night watching the sky and being awed at the magnificence of the spectacle. We would not want to miss a single minute of the phenomenon. We certainly would not ignore the event.

When we read in the Bible about the marvelous things God has done for us, we should think about them and let the wonder soak in. We cannot expect these blessings as our due. We need to be amazed, astounded and awed by God's mighty power and love. We should allow ourselves to be filled with wonder.

Look at what God has created in nature. How could He have devised something as delightful and intricate as a rose? Look at all the stars in the expanse of the night sky, and realize that each one is a sun. Most of them are even larger and brighter than our own sun. Yet God created each one of them, and His great power sustains them. His great wisdom planned the whole universe and everything in it.

Then look at something as simple as a monarch butterfly. How can something so fragile, so delicate, fly thousands of miles in hostile wind and weather to find the way to the small area in Mexico where these butterflies spend the winter? Look closely at those beautiful wings. How can they fly that far?

An article titled "Found at Last: the Monarch's Winter Home" in the August 1976 *National Geographic* tells about the migration of the monarch butterflies over thousands of miles. Tagging the butterflies has shown that they can fly 80 miles in one day, at speeds ranging from 10 to 30 miles an hour. One tagged in Minnesota was found near Mexico City.

"As with our understanding of bird migration, awesome voids remain in our knowledge of the monarch's comings and goings. Not the least of the mysteries is how such a fragile, wind-tossed scrap of life can find its way (only once!) across prairies, deserts, mountain valleys, even cities, to this remote pinpoint on the map of Mexico. Certainly some instinct or programming is involved" (p. 173).

God made the butterflies exactly the way He wanted them to be. If He is concerned about something as trivial as butterflies, how much greater is His love and care for us! He is even more concerned that we find our right way through this world. He will guide and help us even more than He does the butterflies. Do not simply accept this truth, wonder at it!

Everything in the universe proclaims to us the power of God. Everything shows His glory. Everything in the skies should make us feel the awe and reverence appropriate to the mighty Creator of it all. Psalm 19:1-4 makes it plain that all of us can read this revelation about God, no matter what language we speak:

> The heavens declare the glory of God;
> the skies proclaim the work of his hands.
> Day after day they pour forth speech;
> night after night they display knowledge.
> There is no speech or language
> where their voice is not heard.
> Their voice goes out into all the earth,
> their words to the ends of the world.

In the same psalm, verses 7-11 bring us back to God's plans for our worthy living:

> The law of the Lord is perfect,
> reviving the soul.
> The statutes of the Lord are trustworthy,
> making wise the simple.
> The precepts of the Lord are right,
> giving joy to the heart.
> The commands of the Lord are radiant,
> giving light to the eyes.
> The fear of the Lord is pure,
> enduring forever.
> The ordinances of the Lord are sure
> and altogether righteous.
> They are more precious than gold,
> than much pure gold;
> they are sweeter than honey,
> than honey from the comb.
> By them is your servant warned;
> in keeping them there is great reward.

The magnificence of nature truly awes us, but even more awe-inspiring are the spiritual blessings God showers upon us. What could be more awe-full than our salvation that was bought with the blood of Christ Himself!

> Since you call on a Father who judges each man's
> work impartially, live your lives as strangers here
> in reverent fear. For you know that it was not with

> perishable things such as silver or gold that you
> were redeemed from the empty way of life handed
> down to you from your forefathers, but with the
> precious blood of Christ, a lamb without blemish
> or defect. (1 Peter 1:17-19)

The awe Paul felt when he thought of God's love and power is obvious in his prayer in Ephesians 3:16-21:

> I pray that out of his glorious riches he may
> strengthen you with power through his Spirit in
> your inner being, so that Christ may dwell in your
> hearts through faith. And I pray that you, being
> rooted and established in love, may have power, to-
> gether with all the saints, to grasp how wide and
> long and high and deep is the love of Christ, and
> to know this love that surpasses knowledge – that
> you may be filled to the measure of all the fullness
> of God.
> Now to him who is able to do immeasurably
> more than all we ask or imagine, according to his
> power that is at work within us, to him be glory in
> the church and in Christ Jesus throughout all gen-
> erations, for ever and ever! Amen.

The Bible is filled with reasons why we should fear the Lord, reverence Him, stand in awe of Him. Would that our hearts could always overflow with awe and reverence for Him as we try to live our lives worthily!

Awe-Full Reactions

The Bible has many examples of people confronted with awe-inspiring situations. How did they react? What do you think you would have done in the same circumstances?

Zechariah was serving in the temple when an angel told him his aged wife would have a baby. He questioned the angel and lost the power of speech until after the baby was born. Only when he named the baby John according to the angel's directions was Zechariah again able to speak and praise God. Luke 1:65 gives the reaction of the people who witnessed this:

The neighbors were all filled with awe, and throughout the hill country of Judea people were talking about all these things.

When Jesus was born, an angel announced the good news to the shepherds. Although the shepherds were terrified, the angel told them not to be afraid (Luke 2:9-10). Then Luke tells us of their reactions to this announcement:

So they hurried off and found Mary and Joseph, and the baby, who was lying in the manger. When they had seen him, they spread the word concerning what had been told them about this child, and all who heard it were amazed at what the shepherds said to them. But Mary treasured up all these things and pondered them in her heart. The shepherds returned, glorifying and praising God for all the things they had heard and seen, which were just as they had been told. (vv. 16-20)

Jesus healed a paralyzed man by telling him his sins were forgiven. Those witnessing this incident thought Jesus was blaspheming, but He assured them that He had the authority on earth to forgive sins. Then He instructed the man to get up and carry home the mat on which he had been lying. "When the crowd saw this, they were filled with awe; and they praised God, who had given such authority to men" (Matthew 9:8).

Peter, James and John saw the radiance of Jesus with Moses and Elijah at the transfiguration. They heard the voice of God Himself acknowledging Jesus as His Son. "When the disciples heard this, they fell face down to the ground, terrified" (Matthew 17:6).

Just outside the town of Nain, Jesus raised a widow's son from death. The mourners "were all filled with awe and praised God. 'A great prophet has appeared among us,' they said. 'God has come to help his people' " (Luke 7:16).

As Jesus was passing through a crowd, a woman touched the hem of His garment thinking she could be healed in that way. Indeed, she was healed immediately. Jesus recognized the difference between her deliberate touch and the accidental ones of the jostling crowd. When He insisted on being told who had touched His clothes, the woman knew she could not hide from Him. "Then the woman, knowing what had happened to her, came and fell at his feet and, trembling with fear, told him the whole truth" (Mark 5:33).

At the death and resurrection of Jesus several awe-inspiring events occurred. The curtain of the temple was torn from top to bottom, the earth shook, rocks split, tombs broke open, bodies were raised to life and came out of the tombs (Matthew 27:51-52). Even those people who had not previously believed on Jesus could not ignore what happened. Matthew 27:54 tells the reactions of some. "When the centurion and those with him who were guarding Jesus saw the earthquake and all that had happened, they were terrified, and exclaimed, 'Surely he was the Son of God!' "

There was an earthquake on the morning of the resurrection of Jesus when the angel rolled back the stone. The angel spoke to the women who came to the tomb and told them not to be afraid. In Matthew 28:4, 8 we find the reactions of the guards and of the women. "The guards were so afraid of him that they shook and became like dead men. ... So the women hurried away from the tomb, afraid yet filled with joy, and ran to tell his disciples."

Proper fear of the Lord helps us to choose to do right. However, if we are overcome with fear, we may choose to do something really foolish, like asking Jesus to leave us. This was the reaction of some in Luke 8:35-37:

> When they came to Jesus, they found the man from whom the demons had gone out, sitting at Jesus' feet, dressed and in his right mind; and they were afraid. Those who had seen it told the people how the demon-possessed man had been cured. Then all the people of the region of the Gerasenes asked Jesus to leave them, because they were overcome with fear. So he got into the boat and left.

The disciples were wiser than the people of the region of the Gerasenes. When the disciples saw someone walking on the water, they were terrified. However, when they realized that it was Jesus, they willingly accepted Him into the boat with them (John 6:19-21).

In Acts 9:31 we have an important clue concerning why the church spread so rapidly in the first century. "Then the church throughout Judea, Galilee and Samaria enjoyed a time of peace. It was strengthened; and encouraged by the Holy Spirit, it grew in numbers, living in the fear of the Lord." Perhaps our churches, too, would grow in numbers if we lived more in the fear of the Lord.

We have looked at only a few of the many awe-inspiring situations recorded in the Bible. We have seen that people reacted in various ways when they felt this awe. Sometimes awe produced mixed emotions. The miracles of Jesus and the apostles were both amazing and bewildering. Some people believed on God and told others about Him. The most common response was to praise God. Another response was to fall down prostrate before Him. Some fainted, and some fled in terror. Some admitted the truth or confessed their sins. However, the results of those miracles were only temporary. Those healed and resurrected still faced physical death. Although these miracles were amazing and extraordinarily impressive, something greater exists to inspire our awe.

What Christ has done for us is eternal. He has made provisions for our salvation, our eternal life. That is much greater and more awe-inspiring for us than any of the miracles recorded in the Bible, with the exception of the resurrection of Jesus Himself. Perhaps because our redemption is less visible or openly dramatic than those miracles, we take it for granted and do not dwell on how truly great it is. Yet the consciousness of our salvation should motivate us to greater awe, wonder, amazement and reverence than anything else that has ever happened.

Our awareness of awe and reverence for God should be with us daily, not just at special times. Of course, some of our experiences will be more awe-inspiring than others. There will be mountain peaks as well as valleys in our spiritual lives. Remembering the awe-full feelings experienced on the heights will help us get through the depths that are bound to come. When we think about God and His attributes and allow ourselves to be awed by Him, it will be easier to worship Him as He desires.

In today's world, fear of the Lord has been neglected. The loving, forgiving, accepting side of God has been emphasized (as it should be), but the jealous, wrathful, punishing side has been almost totally ignored (which it should not be). We should recognize our need to fear God as well as our need to claim His love for us. Some people do not believe in hell because they think that a kind, loving God would never send anyone to such a place. However, a just God who hates evil must of necessity punish those who sin.

We are free to choose how we will act. Satan tries to make us do wrong, but we are responsible for our own actions. The decision is ours, but God wants us to be saved, not condemned. Having our hearts filled with awe and reverence will help us choose God's way.

How Is Awe Demonstrated?

When our hearts are filled with awe, we find ways to show the Lord our respect and reverence. Awareness of the awesome nature of God is internal but has outward expression.

Our reverence, or lack of it, is noticeable in our speech. Profanity is not only disrespectful, it is also acting as if we do not believe God exists or that He takes notice of what we say.

In addition to the more obvious curse words, common corruptions of the name of God should not be used by anyone who wants to show respect for Him. Of the many such corruptions some are so common that often people say them without even realizing they are using the Lord's name. Among these words that should not be used are "gee," "golly," "gosh," etc. Webster lists these words as euphemisms for Jesus and God.

One might say, "When I say those words, I don't mean anything by them. They are just expressions." Yet that is the very point – using the name of God without meaning is taking the Lord's name in vain. This is exactly what is condemned by God in Exodus 20:7. "You shall not misuse the name of the Lord your God, for the Lord will not hold anyone guiltless who misuses his name." We should use God's name only when we are respectfully and intentionally talking about Him or to Him. It is a very serious mistake ever to use any form of His name in a thoughtless, meaningless or inappropriate way.

Our reverence is further revealed by our relationships with others. We must realize that all people are made in the image of God. If we despise others, we are also despising the One who made them. The parable in Matthew 25:31-46 depicting the final judgment shows that how we treat others is also how we treat the Lord. When we are filled with awe and thanksgiving because of the many things God has done for us, we must realize that He has also done these same things for others. He loves everyone else just as much as He loves us. Respect for Him demands that we follow His standards of justice and mercy. Our everyday relationships reveal the extent of our awe and reverence for God.

We also show our reverence to God in our desire to pray to Him and in the way we address Him in prayer. Awe balances our boldness to approach God with the recognition of His majesty and power over us.

Our reverence, moreover, is expressed in our attention to the Word of God. If we respect Him, we will want to hear from Him, to know what He says. If we fear Him, we will submit to His words. If we neglect the study of the Bible, we cut ourselves off from the awe that comes from learning more about God.

In summary, our reverence is shown as we try to do our best. If we are half-hearted in our reverence, we will also be half-hearted in our commitments. If we do everything as though we are doing it for God, then we will not be satisfied with less than our best efforts.

Awe-Full Worship

Awe is an essential element in the worship and service of God. If we have never felt this awe, this fear of God, we cannot worship Him acceptably. Obviously we are not able to sustain these deep feelings of reverence and awe every time we want to worship Him. Still, if we continue to acknowledge the awesome nature of God we will be able to approach Him with the proper attitude of adoration.

When we are aware of the holiness and glory of God, we will feel the reverent and holy awe that is appropriate to His magnificence. Both our hearts and our actions will be changed by that awareness. We will not allow ourselves to be casual or flippant in our worship to Him. We will realize the seriousness of being in His presence whether we are alone as we worship Him or whether we are in the company of the community of believers. Although we stand in awe of God, we may still approach Him with the boldness He has allowed us. Although we cannot be careless or unthinking, we can still be familiar and personal. Being aware of God's constant presence will help us to live lives worthy of Him at all times.

One of His most precious promises is that He will always be with us. Because of this and other promises, 2 Corinthians 7:1 tells us "Since we have these promises, dear friends, let us purify ourselves from everything that contaminates body and spirit, perfecting holiness out of reverence for God."

Discussion Questions

1. How would you describe awe, reverence and the fear of God?
2. What difference do you see between fearing God and being afraid of Him? What is the relationship between fear of God and love? How does fearing God affect your life?
3. When you think about all the blessings God gives you and when you think about His power, wisdom and glory, what feelings do you experience? How can you appropriately express these feelings both to God and to your associates?
4. Describe some time in your life when you have been awed by the power of God. Try to describe your feelings.
5. Discuss the attributes of God listed in this chapter and how they influence your life. What other attributes of God are especially meaningful to you?
6. How do feelings of awe, reverence and fear of God influence what you do and how you feel as you worship God, both individually and in assembly with other Christians? How can you help yourself and others to feel the reverence and awe that are a necessary part of worshiping God?
7. In your own prayer life, how do you reconcile the majesty of God with the boldness you have in approaching His throne? How do you feel about having

the privilege of confidently approaching the omnipotent, omniscient, glorious Father in heaven?

8. What are some things in nature that inspire you with awe and wonder? Describe the most beautiful, awe-inspiring thing you have ever seen.

9. What are some spiritual blessings that inspire you with awe and reverence? How do you respond?

10. How do you personally react when you feel awe in the presence of God? How does that awe affect the way you live every day?

11. The Bible has many examples of people confronted with awe-inspiring situations, such as the miracles of Jesus. How did those people react? What did they do? If you had been there, what do you think your reactions would have been?

12. What importance does "that awe-full feeling" hold in your own life?

CHAPTER • 4

$\mathcal{A}$ Chaste Lifestyle

"Be holy because I, the Lord your God,
am holy" (Leviticus 19:2).

Several years ago, in preparation for teaching a series of lessons based on Titus 2:3-5, I asked the class to fill out a questionnaire which included the following question: "When you hear the word, 'chaste,' which members of our group do you think of and why?"

One person suggested some names then added, "For the obvious reason, of course."

However, is the meaning of "chaste" really that obvious? How long has it been since you heard the word in conversation? Why do you suppose it is so rarely used? Is it merely one of those old-fashioned words going out of style, or is the word rare because the concept behind it is becoming rare in today's world? Just what does it mean?

Many people assume that "chaste" refers only to sexual purity, especially on the part of women. However, upon closer inspection, that assumption is not correct. Two passages of Scripture illustrate this point.

The concept of sexual purity is certainly included in Titus 2:4-5: Older women should teach the younger women

> to love their husbands, to love their children, to be
> sober-minded, chaste, workers at home, kind, be-

ing in subjection to their own husbands, that the
word of God be not blasphemed. (ASV)

However, the same Greek word is used in 1 Peter 3:1-2, and
there the meaning cannot logically be limited to sexual purity.

Ye wives, be in subjection to your own husbands;
that, even if any obey not the word, they may without the word be gained by the behavior of their
wives: beholding your chaste behavior coupled with
fear. (ASV)

It is highly unlikely that anyone will ever decide to follow
Christ simply because his wife does not commit adultery.
Limiting the meaning of the word to sexual purity would
make these verses say something not intended in the original. "Chaste" means more than not having sexual intercourse
with someone to whom one is not married.

The English word "chaste" does refer primarily, but not exclusively, to sexual purity. However, the Greek word, while
including this narrow sense of chastity, is broader in meaning and has a different emphasis. Newer translations of the
Bible have recognized the limitations of the word "chaste"
and have more accurately translated the Greek by the English
word "pure," or "purity," as in the New International Version:

Wives, in the same way be submissive to your husbands so that, if any of them do not believe the
word, they may be won over without talk by the
behavior of their wives, when they see the purity
and reverence of your lives. (1 Peter 3:1-2)

So then, what does the Greek word mean? What is a chaste
lifestyle?

What Does "Chaste" Mean?

The Greek word translated "chaste" or "pure" is *hagnos*. It
means pure, chaste, holy, hallowed, undefiled, guiltless or upright. This word is closely related, in meaning as well as in
spelling, to *hagios*, which means "holy." Originally *hagnos* referred to something holy: something that is characteristic of
deity and/or belonging to deity, or to something that inspires

religious awe. It also refers to ritual purity and strict observance of religious duties. This includes the idea of chastity, of being undefiled and guiltless. It also contains the idea of integrity. The verb form means to cleanse, to purify or to consecrate.

In the Septuagint, the ancient Greek translation of the Old Testament, *hagnos* was used to translate two different Hebrew words, one of which means "ritually pure" and the other "morally upright." Thus we see that this Greek word means not only performing the proper ceremonial acts prescribed by God but also having the moral conduct expected by God.

The more common Greek word translated "pure" or "clean" is *katharos*, which is a more general word. It refers to physical cleansing as well as to both ritual and moral purity. The distinctive nuance of *hagnos* is integrity.

Three Types of Purity

The Bible applies the idea of purity on three levels: ceremonial, moral and religious. Perhaps looking at all three will help us to understand better the meanings of chaste and pure.

The Old Testament has much to say about ceremonial purity, or cleanness. This has to do with the difference between what is clean and unclean for ritual purposes. Leviticus 11-15 defines what is clean and unclean and gives instructions concerning purification from the unclean. Details are given of specific things that must be done in certain ways in order to satisfy God's requirements of ceremonial purity.

Leviticus 5:2 contains another reference to ceremonial purity:

> If a person touches anything ceremonially unclean
> – whether the carcasses of unclean wild animals or
> of unclean livestock or of unclean creatures that
> move along the ground – even though he is un-
> aware of it, he has become unclean and is guilty.

Verses 5-13 of the same chapter describe exactly how to receive forgiveness for that guilt. The guilty person first confessed what was done. Then, as a penalty for that sin, a sacrifice of a specific animal was offered to God. If one could not afford the lamb or goat required, the Lord allowed certain less expensive sacrifices. However, in order to make atonement, the priest was required to follow precisely the orders given by God concerning the way the animal was killed, what was done with the blood and other prescribed rituals.

Thus we see that ritual purity meant accurately following explicit instructions regarding ceremonies that must be observed. Perhaps God insisted upon this ceremonial purity in order to teach the people distinctions and so to lead them to the concept of moral purity.

Moral purity is also required to please God. This kind of purity refers to the differences between what is morally right and what is morally wrong. It means obedience to the moral or ethical laws of God. For example: do not steal; do not lie (Exodus 20:15-16). It is possible for one to obey these laws even if the heart is not involved – the motives can be wrong. For example, one could tell the truth, not simply because it is the right thing to do but because in that particular instance being truthful would be in one's own best interests. So, although moral purity – telling the truth – might be present, something important – purity of heart – would still be lacking.

A third type of purity might be defined as religious purity, spiritual integrity, or whole-hearted devotion to God. This refers to a comprehensive distinction between what is the will of God and what is not. It involves doing what God wants, not merely because it is seen as one's duty or corresponds to some human standard of right and wrong but, more importantly, because one loves God and wants to please Him in every way. The heart and the motives are attuned to God and His will.

We cannot equate, on the one hand, the ritual with what is outward and, on the other hand, the moral with what is inward. Although the ceremonial rites are external and seen by others, the inner being must also be involved. Doing the morally correct thing does not necessarily mean the heart and motives are right. To have total purity before God, we must do whatever outward forms God has commanded exactly as He tells us; we must distinguish between right and wrong to the best of our abilities doing only what is morally right, and we must give our hearts to God in love, wanting to obey and please Him in everything.

Obedience from the Heart

We are sometimes told that in the Old Testament God was concerned that His laws be obeyed to the letter, while in the New Testament He wants us to get our hearts right with Him. However, this distinction is not accurate. God was just as concerned in the Old Testament with the hearts of His people as He is with ours, and He wants us to obey Him as completely as He wanted their obedience.

Under the Law given to Moses on Mount Sinai, God wanted His people to serve Him with their hearts.

> And now, O Israel, what does the Lord your God ask of you but to fear the Lord your God, to walk in all his ways, to love him, to serve the Lord your God with all your heart and with all your soul, and to observe the Lord's commands and decrees that I am giving you today for your own good? (Deuteronomy 10:12-13)

In the Great Commission, Jesus insisted on total obedience.

> Then Jesus came to them and said, "All authority in heaven and on earth has been given to me. Therefore go and make disciples of all nations, baptizing them in the name of the Father and of the Son and of the Holy Spirit, and teaching them to obey everything I have commanded you. And surely I will be with you always, to the very end of the age."(Matthew 28:18-20)

God has always been concerned that His people have pure hearts and serve Him fully. He has never been satisfied with merely external obedience that does not come from the heart. It took, and still takes, outward purity of actions, inner purity of motives, and total commitment of heart to please God. It has never been enough that God's people just be clean ritually and morally; He has always wanted total purity from His people.

In accordance with these three types of purity, the word translated "chaste" is not limited to sexual purity but refers to purity and integrity in all aspects of our lives: ethics, thoughts, motives, relationships, actions and everything else. In the discussion of the meaning of *hagnos*, *The Vocabulary of the Greek Testament* by Moulton and Milligan states, "The adjective and its derivatives may ... take a wide meaning, as wide as our *pure* in the ethical sense. But a starting-point must not be overlooked: ... it originally denoted 'in a condition prepared for worship'" (London: Hodder & Stoughton, 1952, p. 5).

Worship under the old law involved animal sacrifice. To be acceptable to God, the animals offered had to be pure, without any defects or blemishes. "Do not sacrifice to the Lord your God an ox or a sheep that has any defect or flaw in it, for that would be detestable to him" (Deuteronomy 17:1; see also Leviticus 22:17-25; Deuteronomy 15:21). Under the new law, worship still involves sacrifices that must be pure. The difference is that now we, not animals, are the sacrifices. Christians are urged "to offer your bodies as living sacrifices, holy and pleasing to God – which is your spiritual worship" (Romans 12:1). In order to be in a condition ready to worship God, we who sacrifice ourselves under the new law must be as spotless and pure as the sacrifices required under the old law.

Verses That Use *hagnos*

Examining the verses in the New Testament that use a form of *hagnos* will help us understand the word better, and understanding the word better will enrich our understanding of what it means to be chaste. In the following quotations from the Bible, the words in italics are those that translate a form of the Greek word *hagnos*.

Ritual Purity

The New Testament continues to use the word for "chaste" in reference to the purification rituals of the Jewish people. The verb form occurs in John 11:55. "When it was almost time for the Jewish Passover, many went up from the country to Jerusalem for their *ceremonial cleansing* [literally, 'in order that they might *cleanse* themselves'] before the Passover."

The Jews were required to perform specific rituals and meet certain conditions in order to take part in the Passover feast. John 18:28 tells us that at the time of the trial of Jesus before the Roman governor, "to avoid ceremonial uncleanness the

Jews did not enter the palace; they wanted to be able to eat the Passover." They were careful to remain pure ceremonially, but in their hearts they were planning murder.

Both verb and noun forms of *hagnos* are used in Acts 21:24 and 26, when the leaders of the church in Jerusalem advised Paul to avoid criticism from the Jews by following certain Jewish ceremonies:

> Take these men, join in their *purification rites* and pay their expenses, so that they can have their heads shaved. Then everybody will know there is no truth in these reports about you, but that you yourself are living in obedience to the law. ... The next day Paul took the men and *purified* himself along with them. Then he went to the temple to give notice of the date when the days of *purification* would end and the offering would be made for each of them.

In Acts 24:18 Paul refers to his visit to the temple after these purification rites. "I was *ceremonially clean* when they found me in the temple courts." Paul followed the Old Testament purification code even though it was no longer necessary for him to do so. He did it in order to be able to gain a hearing from the ritually observant Jews for his message about Christ.

Purity of Heart

Purification ceremonies such as those Paul underwent were required by God under the old law. He used that law to prepare people for the new law. Although He no longer requires the same temple sacrifices and ceremonies, He does still require purity of His people. He still wants us to make the distinctions that those laws taught people to make. The ways to attain the required purity may be less visible than those under the old law, but they are just as necessary and just as personal.

James 4:8 tells us of the necessity of cleansing our hearts from sin. "Come near to God and he will come near to you. Wash your hands, you sinners, and *purify* your hearts, you double-minded." Although we are sinners, we must try to be pure. Notice the change from outer, concrete actions of the purification rites to the inner symbolic, total action of purifying the heart.

A number of scriptures help us understand how to purify our hearts.

In his first letter to the church in Corinth, Paul corrected some things that they were doing wrong. He touched their hearts as he told them what they should do and how they should act. In 2 Corinthians 7:11 he refers to their reaction to his earlier letter:

> See what this godly sorrow has produced in you: what earnestness, what eagerness to clear yourselves, what indignation, what alarm, what longing, what concern, what readiness to see justice done. At every point you have proved yourselves to be *innocent* in this matter.

His earlier words had hurt them because they saw their own faults, but they turned that hurt to godly sorrow and repented of the things they were doing wrong. They tried their best to correct their faults. Their attitude and actions showed that they were again pure and morally blameless.

Notice the words Paul used to show how determined the Corinthian Christians were to correct their wrongs: earnestness, eagerness, indignation, alarm, longing, concern, readiness to see justice done. When they saw what God wanted them to do, they did what they could to make themselves pure and innocent. They changed their ways. They had been sinning, but Paul's previous letter made them sorry. They repented, and this godly sorrow made them pure again. That is why they were morally blameless or innocent, and that is the kind of repentance God wants of us, also.

We do not always do what is right; we do not always follow God's will. However, when we read the Bible and see that we are not following all of God's will for us, we can repent, change what we are doing, and become innocent, or pure. We must not give up trying to do right just because we have made a mistake, no matter how serious that mistake is. God can and will forgive us and make us pure and holy again in His sight.

We are assured of this forgiveness in 1 John 1:5-10:

> This is the message we have heard from him and declare to you: God is light; in him there is no dark-

ness at all. If we claim to have fellowship with him yet walk in the darkness, we lie and do not live by the truth. But if we walk in the light, as he is in the light, we have fellowship with one another, and the blood of Jesus, his Son, purifies us from every sin. If we claim to be without sin, we deceive ourselves and the truth is not in us. If we confess our sins, he is faithful and just and will forgive us our sins and purify us from all unrighteousness. If we claim we have not sinned, we make him out to be a liar and his word has no place in our lives.

Our forgiveness comes from God through the blood of Christ, but we must show our repentance by the way we live.

Chaste in Thought and Deed

The company a word keeps is an important pointer to the kinds of things included and the associations of the word. Philippians 4:8 uses several words connected with purity:

Finally, brothers, whatever is true, whatever is noble, whatever is right, whatever is *pure*, whatever is lovely, whatever is admirable – if anything is excellent or praiseworthy – think about such things.

We need to fill our minds with the kind of thoughts that are listed here. When improper thoughts come into our minds, we can push them out by thinking about things that are good and pure.

After urging us to think about these good things, verse 9 insists that we also practice them. It is not enough merely to have the opinion that these things are good; we must act on them. Our daily activities must be the expression of the good and pure thoughts in our minds.

On the other hand, if we allow our thoughts to be wrong, sin will follow. "For out of the heart come evil thoughts, murders, adultery, sexual immorality, theft, false testimony, slander" (Matthew 15:19). Evil thoughts lead to evil actions.

It is very important to control our thoughts and to keep them pure and good. Proverbs 4:23 gives a reason for this importance. "Above all else, guard your heart, for it is the wellspring of life." Out of the thoughts of our hearts come the actions of our lives, whether good or evil. If our thoughts and motives are pure it is more likely that our actions will be pure also. Thought precedes action. When we act without conscious thought, we function as a result of prior conditioning. Thus it is important that we keep our minds tuned to right thinking so that we will react in the right way.

Careless thoughts lead to careless actions. Therefore we must think, or plan, to do what is right in order to accomplish what is right. We must control what is in our minds, because our thoughts determine to a great extent the kind of persons that we are. "For as he thinketh within himself, so is he" (Proverbs 23:7 ASV).

Perhaps we cannot avoid having bad thoughts come into our minds, but we do not have to dwell on them. We must push bad thoughts out of our minds by substituting good thoughts. We must deliberately think about something true, noble, right, pure, lovely, admirable, excellent or praiseworthy. We incorporate these things into our lives by first thinking about them, then acting according to them. We must think good thoughts and follow those good thoughts with good actions.

Timothy was instructed to set an example for others by the things that he did. "Don't let anyone look down on you because you are young, but set an example for the believers in speech, in life, in love, in faith and in *purity*" (1 Timothy 4:12). Again we learn something about the meaning of the word by the company it keeps. Purity must permeate these other aspects of life, otherwise they would not be useful as examples. Facets of purity emphasized here include purity of speech, conduct, relationships and faith. Sexual purity is included as part of the relationships to others: "Treat younger men as brothers, older women as mothers, and younger women as sisters, with absolute *purity*" (1 Timothy 5:1-2). The directives concerning purity of conduct continue: "[D]o not share in the sins of others. Keep yourself *pure*" (v. 22).

'Chaste' Includes Sexual Purity

Although the idea of sexual purity is crucial in 2 Corinthians 11:2-3, it is only one element of the larger meaning of the concept of purity:

> I am jealous for you with a godly jealousy. I
> promised you to one husband, to Christ, so that I
> might present you as a *pure* virgin to him. But I am
> afraid that just as Eve was deceived by the serpent's
> cunning, your minds may somehow be led astray
> from your sincere and *pure* devotion to Christ.

The word "virgin" carries with it the idea of sexual purity,
but the modifier "pure" indicates more than merely "virgin."
It is not enough that we, both men and women, be presented
to Christ in a sexually pure state, but also that we be pure in
other aspects of our lives. In the context of this passage Paul
rebukes the Corinthians for following teachers who intro-
duced things other than the gospel of Christ as the standard
of teaching. Our moral and sexual purity is an expression of
our whole-hearted devotion to Christ and His gospel.

Two passages we have already mentioned include the idea
of sexual purity while extending that purity to all of life. Titus
2:3-5 has instructions for women in various stages of their lives:

> Likewise, teach the older women to be reverent in
> the way they live, not to be slanderers or addict-
> ed to much wine, but to teach what is good. Then
> they can train the younger women to love their
> husbands and children, to be self-controlled and
> *pure*, to be busy at home, to be kind, and to be sub-
> ject to their husbands, so that no one will malign
> the word of God.

Purity must be a part of all these areas of life in order for
one to live up to the standards set forth here.

First Peter 3:1-4 also shows the importance of a chaste
lifestyle:

> Wives, in the same way be submissive to your hus-
> bands so that, if any of them do not believe the
> word, they may be won over without talk by the
> behavior of their wives, when they see the *purity*
> and reverence of your lives. Your beauty should not
> come from outward adornment, such as braided
> hair and the wearing of gold jewelry and fine

clothes. Instead, it should be that of your inner self, the unfading beauty of a gentle and quiet spirit, which is of great worth in God's sight.

The importance of the purity of the inner self, which is the heart or the mind, is emphasized here. We are what we are in our hearts, not how we look or what we wear on the outside. In both of these passages our morality is linked to our relationship to God.

Another consideration is that purity is an attribute of wisdom. There is worldly wisdom, and there is heavenly wisdom. James discusses both, then spells out the latter. "But the wisdom that comes from heaven is first of all *pure*; then peace loving, considerate, submissive, full of mercy and good fruit, impartial and sincere" (3:17). Purity of life results in peaceful, considerate and submissive conduct. On the other hand, selfishness and envy lead to discord and bitterness. The wisdom that is pure and holy comes from God, while the so-called wisdom that comes from the devil is the opposite (vv. 13-18.)

"Chaste" Includes Sincerity and Love

The idea that sincerity is a part of purity is brought out in Philippians 1:15-18. Paul uses a form of the word for purity to describe the motivation of some contemporary preachers who lacked integrity:

> It is true that some preach Christ out of envy and rivalry, but others out of good will. The latter do so in love, knowing that I am put here for the defense of the gospel. The former preach Christ out of selfish ambition, not *sincerely*, supposing that they can stir up trouble for me while I am in chains. But what does it matter? The important thing is that in every way, whether from false motives or true, Christ is preached.

Even someone whose heart is not pure can accomplish something good. But how much better it would be for that person if he has a pure and sincere heart.

First Peter 1:22 tells us how to purify our hearts. "Now that you have *purified* yourselves by obeying the truth so that you have sincere love for your brothers, love one another deeply, from the heart." How can we purify ourselves? By obeying God. How do we show this in our lives? By loving our fellow Christians. Our purity is shown in the way we treat others. Purity in our relationships is vital.

The love that is described here is not a warm, fuzzy feeling. It is not emotion but action. It is the way we act toward other individuals. We treat them with respect, with caring, with tenderness, and with consideration. We treat them the way we would like to be treated. We want what is best for them. We do not lie to others, but we are honest and above-board with everyone. Our love for others must be sincere, from our hearts, and not self-serving.

The next verse, 1 Peter 1:23, gives the motivation for this kind of love. "For you have been born again, not of perishable seed, but of imperishable, through the living and enduring word of God." It is because of God that we should live in a worthy manner. It is because of God's holiness that we should be holy. It is because of God's love for us that we should love others. It is because God has saved us that we should respond in obedience to His word. It is because of God's purity that our hearts should be pure and sincere. It is because of the word of God that we know Him and what He wants of us.

First John 3:1-3 also contains the idea that our lives should be lived in response to God and what He has done for us:

> How great is the love the Father has lavished on us, that we should be called children of God! And that is what we are! The reason the world does not know us is that it did not know him. Dear friends, now we are children of God, and what we will be has not yet been made known. But we know that when he appears, we shall be like him, for we shall see him as he is. Everyone who has this hope in him *purifies* himself, just as he is *pure*.

Hope purifies. The hope of being with God in eternity gives us the purpose for our lives. We want to purify ourselves because God is pure.

Focus on Purity

Having a single-minded goal keeps us focused and prevents extraneous matters from corrupting or diverting us from living worthy lives. It has been said that "Purity of heart is to will one thing."

Consider an archer who looks at the target, carefully aiming at it while shutting out of his sight everything but the center of that target. This focused archer is much more likely to hit the mark than one who merely points his arrow somewhere in the general direction of the target and lets the arrow fly. The second archer could not reasonably expect the arrow to hit the bull's eye, whereas the first archer has great hope that the arrow will accurately find its goal. In the same way, we must focus on the goal of purity in order to realize the hope that God has offered us.

Psalm 86:11 expresses the ideas of being obedient to God and having a single-minded purpose in our lives:

> Teach me your way, O Lord,
>   and I will walk in your truth;
> give me an undivided heart,
>   that I may fear your name.

If one's heart is divided in its loyalties, one cannot aim whole-heartedly at the goal of living a worthy life and enjoying the hope of eternal life with God. A heart undivided in its faithfulness to God will allow us to incorporate into our lives the fear, the awe and the reverence that are due Him.

From these scriptures we can see that being chaste or pure is not limited to sexual purity, but certainly includes it. If one's thoughts, motives, desires and priorities are kept pure, then one's lifestyle will also be pure.

Whole-Life Purity

As we have seen from the verses that use a form of the Greek word *hagnos*, purity includes the totality of our lives: our thoughts (Philippians 4:8; Proverbs 4:23), our actions (1 Timothy 5:22; Titus 2:3-5; 1 Peter 3:1-4), our motives (Philippians 1:15-18; 1 John 3:1-3), our ethics (James 3:17), our intentions

(2 Corinthians 11:2-3), our relationships (1 Timothy 5:1-2; 1 Peter 1:22), our sexuality (2 Corinthians 11:2-3; 1 Timothy 5:1-2; Titus 2:3-5), everything (1 Timothy 4:12; James 3:17).

There is no room in our lives for anything that is against God and His way: duplicity, manipulation, lying (even little white lies), cheating, stealing (even taking supplies from the office for personal use), etc. Commitment to Christ demands that we commit the totality of our lives to Him. A chaste lifestyle includes everything about us, inner as well as outer.

Notice the areas of our lives mentioned in Ephesians 4:17-5:1:

> So I tell you this, and insist on it in the Lord, that you must no longer live as the Gentiles do, in the futility of their thinking. They are darkened in their understanding and separated from the life of God because of the ignorance that is in them due to the hardening of their hearts. Having lost all sensitivity, they have given themselves over to sensuality so as to indulge in every kind of impurity, with a continual lust for more.
>
> ... You were taught, with regard to your former way of life, to put off your old self, which is being corrupted by its deceitful desires; to be made new in the attitude of your minds; and to put on the new self, created to be like God in true righteousness and holiness.
>
> Therefore each of you must put off falsehood and speak truthfully to his neighbor, for we are all members of one body. "In your anger do not sin": Do not let the sun go down while you are still angry, and do not give the devil a foothold. He who has been stealing must steal no longer, but must work, doing something useful with his own hands, that he may have something to share with those in need.
>
> Do not let any unwholesome talk come out of your mouths, but only what is helpful for building others up according to their needs, that it may benefit those who listen. And do not grieve the Holy Spirit of God, with whom you were sealed for the

day of redemption. Get rid of all bitterness, rage and anger, brawling and slander, along with every form of malice. Be kind and compassionate to one another, forgiving each other, just as in Christ God forgave you.

Be imitators of God, therefore, as dearly loved children and live a life of love, just as Christ loved us and gave himself up for us as a fragrant offering and sacrifice to God.

The thought processes of Christians must be different from those of the people who do not know God. We must not be ignorant of God; our hearts must not be hardened against Him. We must be sensitive to doing what is right rather than following our lusts. Our attitudes must be right. We should realize that we were created to be like God in His holiness and righteousness. Our speech must be truthful and honest. We must control our tempers. We must not steal but do an honest day's work. We must think of others and be ready to help them. We must eliminate impurities in our lives in order to imitate God and show in our lives the kind of love for others that Christ showed us. Thus we see that our minds, our hearts, our sensitivities, our desires, our motivation, our attitudes, our speech, our tempers, our work ethic, our relationships, and our devotion to God must all be pure. Our entire lifestyle should be in keeping with the purity and holiness of God.

Purity and Holiness

Purity is closely related to holiness. God's holiness demands that we, too, be holy as we approach Him. Because sin separates us from God, we cannot come before Him while still clinging to our sins. We must turn away from sin in order to draw closer to God. As we come closer to Him, He also comes closer to us (James 4:7-10).

The Bible emphasizes the necessity of imitating God's holiness and making it the motivation for our actions. "The Lord said to Moses, 'Speak to the entire assembly of Israel and say to them: "Be holy because I, the Lord your God, am holy" ' " (Leviticus 19:1-2). Although these words were spoken to a large group of people, the holiness demanded here is personal. Each person must be holy in order for the entire nation to be holy. This fact can be illustrated by the story of Achan in Joshua 7. Because of the sin of one man, the entire nation suffered a defeat at the first battle of Ai. Only when the impurity was completely purged from the nation was the next battle successful.

Peter quoted Leviticus 19:2 in his discussion of Christianity and what it means:

> Therefore, prepare your minds for action; be self-controlled; set your hope fully on the grace to be given you when Jesus Christ is revealed. As obedient children, do not conform to the evil desires you had when you lived in ignorance. But just as he who called you is holy, so be holy in all you do; for it is written: "Be holy, because I am holy." (1 Peter 1:13-16)

Again we see that our holiness is dependent upon and motivated by God and His holiness.

Without purity there can be no holiness. One cannot be holy and impure at the same time. Because holiness is at the very center of Christianity, we must be careful to strive for holiness in everything that we do. In 2 Peter 3:11, 14 we find the admonitions "to live holy and godly lives. ... [M]ake every effort to be found spotless, blameless and at peace with him." In striving for holiness we receive purity. Because our holiness must be total, even our moral and ethical activities are given a religious meaning.

The Standard of Purity

What is the standard by which to measure the purity of our lives? Customs? Traditions? Our peer groups? The media? What everyone else is doing?

We may be tempted to judge the level of our purity against what we see around us: what others are doing or what is on television and in the movies. "If everyone else is doing it, it must be all right."

We may look around and see that others are less pure than we consider ourselves, so we feel self-righteous. "If I am better than others, then I must be all right." We may think, "It's always been done this way, so it must be all right." None of these criteria is valid.

The only standard by which we can measure ourselves is Christ as He is revealed to us in the Bible. Philippians 2:5 has an important admonition for us. "Your attitude should be the same as that of Christ Jesus." What was that attitude? Was it that He would go along with the crowd and follow peer pressure? Would He look down on others as not being worth as much as He? Would He rely on the customs and traditions of the people around him? How does the Bible describe Christ's attitude?

> Who, being in very nature God,
>   did not consider equality with God something to
>   be grasped,
> but made himself nothing,
>   taking the very nature of a servant,
>   being made in human likeness.
> And being found in appearance as a man,
>   he humbled himself
>   and became obedient to death –
>   even death on a cross! (vv. 6-8)

Although Jesus was equal with God, He came to this earth and lived as a human being, serving others. He had the attitude of humility and obedience. He lived a life of perfect purity. He exemplified the standard of excellence for us in purity, in obedience, in submission, and in everything else. Our goal must be to be like Him.

How can Christians have the same attitude that Christ had? On the one hand, we ought to think of ourselves as nothing: Christ, being equal to God, made Himself nothing in order to be like us. On the other hand, we ought to think of ourselves as something special and precious: look at what Christ did for us and how much He loves us! He has enabled us to be children of the holy and almighty God and Father in heaven! We are princes and princesses, priests and priestesses (1 Peter 2:9); and that is very special. Yet we must remember that our specialness is not to our personal credit; we have done absolutely nothing to deserve this great honor and glory. It is only because of God's unsurpassable love for us that we receive His mercy and grace.

Christ must be our absolute standard of purity. Surely we want to live lives worthy of Him by keeping that standard before us as the pattern for our lives.

If we exhibit in our lives the validity of this standard, those around us will recognize it. We bring glory to God when people observe Christ living through us. If, however, we do not try to live up to what we claim to believe, then our associates will notice that, too. We cannot merely tell others what God wants us to do; we must also behave in a way that reveals, without flaunting, the humility, obedience to God, and purity of our lives. We must be pure and chaste as we try to live worthily for God.

What Should We Avoid to Be Chaste?

An important part of a chaste lifestyle is knowing what to avoid. First Thessalonians 5:22 states very concisely a vital principle. "Avoid every kind of evil."

A key word here is "avoid." Stay as far away as possible from every form of wrongdoing. Sometimes we try to flirt with temptations, just to show how strong we are. However, we must resist evil. We must not put ourselves in a place of temptation, thinking, "Oh, I can handle it. It won't affect me." Perhaps if David had not been on the rooftop, he would not have seen Bathsheba and thus been tempted (2 Samuel 11). He would have avoided a lot of trouble if he had been wise enough to leave the area immediately when he caught sight of her.

Another key word in 1 Thessalonians 5:22 is "every." This does not refer to whatever merely seems to look bad. Rather it means that every time evil appears, we must avoid it. Although this passage does not refer specifically to that which might look as if it is wrong, it is still a good policy to avoid anything that even appears to be wrong. We must consistently shun anything and everything that is opposed to God.

Another passage that teaches us to avoid evil is Ephesians 5:3-7. No one should be able to identify that wrongdoing is present in our lives.

> You are God's people, so don't let it be said that any of you are immoral or indecent or greedy. Don't use dirty or foolish or filthy words. Instead, say how thankful you are. Being greedy, indecent, or immoral is just another way of worshiping idols. You can be sure that people who behave in this way will never be part of the kingdom that belongs to Christ and to God. Don't let anyone trick you with foolish talk. God punishes everyone who disobeys him and says foolish things. So don't have anything to do with anyone like that. (CEB)

Not only should we avoid immorality, impurity, and idolatry; we should also distance ourselves from people who practice such things. It is true that we must have some kind of contact with wrongdoers in order to persuade them of God's way, but we must not allow ourselves to become participants with them. We must not encourage them or seem to give approval to their activities.

The Bible gives us ample information concerning things that are opposed to purity and holiness. Several passages in the Bible give us lists of things to avoid. One is Revelation 21:8. "But the cowardly, the unbelieving, the vile, the murderers, the sexually immoral, those who practice magic arts, the idolaters and all liars – their place will be in the fiery lake of burning sulfur. This is the second death." We may find it easy to avoid some of these things. However, many of us wish that "all liars" had not been included. We would like to think that "It's okay to tell something that is not quite true if I don't really mean it and if nobody gets hurt by it." When we bend the truth, sooner or later it will become obvious to others, and they will lose respect for our integrity. They will no longer trust us. Any untruthfulness that we speak damages our credibility and keeps us from being pure in thought, speech and motives. If we continue to practice these sins, our punishment will be certain.

Satan is alive and well and continues to work against us. He tries to control our thoughts as well as our actions. He is an old pro, and we are novices. Even if we have been fighting against Satan for 50 years or more, we are still beginners compared to him. Satan knows all the tricks and has practiced them until he has them perfected. Every one of his temptations is new to us. Every time we figure out how to counteract him, he has already chosen his next tactic, which again is new to us. On the other hand, God has been observing Satan from the very beginning. Nothing that Satan can do is new to God. Therefore we need help from God to fight against Satan's temptations. Only with God's help can we overcome the evil influences surrounding us.

Flesh Versus Spirit

Galatians 5 also tells us some things to avoid. This passage contrasts what we should not do with what we should do. The two lists contained here are sometimes labeled "fruit of the flesh" and "fruit of the Spirit." However, this is not quite what the Bible calls them. The first list is not the "fruit" but the "acts" or "works" of the flesh: it enumerates things we should not do. The second, the "fruit of the Spirit," identifies qualities – that is, not just what we do but what we are. Looking at verses 19-26 in this way gives us a little more insight into the meaning:

> The acts of the sinful nature are obvious: sexual immorality, impurity and debauchery; idolatry and witchcraft; hatred, discord, jealousy, fits of rage, selfish ambition, dissensions, factions and envy; drunkenness, orgies, and the like. I warn you, as I did before, that those who live like this will not inherit the kingdom of God.
>
> But the fruit of the Spirit is love, joy, peace, patience, kindness, goodness, faithfulness, gentleness and self-control. Against such things there is no law. Those who belong to Christ Jesus have crucified the sinful nature with its passions and desires. Since we live by the Spirit, let us keep in step with the Spirit. Let us not become conceited, provoking and envying each other.

It is, of course, our habitual manner of life that determines what we are and our habitual manner of life is determined by what we do. The fruit of the Spirit is expressed in the qualities that are exhibited to other people by our lives when we continually try to follow God's will. They become our way of life – not just something we decide to do each morning. Like a tree that is recognized as a peach tree when the peaches are ripe, we are recognized by the fruit that we produce in our lives. On the other hand, the sinful nature, the flesh, reveals itself in sinful works.

Verse 25 tells us to "keep in step with the Spirit." This is another way of saying, "Live a life worthy of the Spirit."

A number of other scriptures tell us things to avoid as we try to live worthy lives. We will quote only a few of them.

Proverbs 6:16-19 is explicit in describing some things God does not like:

> There are six things the Lord hates,
>   seven that are detestable to him:
>   haughty eyes,
>   a lying tongue,
>   hands that shed innocent blood,
>   a heart that devises wicked schemes,
>   feet that are quick to rush into evil,
>   a false witness who pours out lies
>   and a man who stirs up dissension among
>   brothers.

Certainly we should avoid anything that the Lord hates.

Romans 13:13-14 reminds us that Jesus must be the motivation for our behavior:

> Let us behave decently, as in the daytime, not in orgies and drunkenness, not in sexual immorality and debauchery, not in dissension and jealousy. Rather, clothe yourselves with the Lord Jesus Christ, and do not think about how to gratify the desires of the sinful nature.

One way to avoid these sins is to avoid thinking about doing them.

Impurity by Association

Second Corinthians 6:14-18 urges us to stay away from associations with unbelievers and people who are unrighteous. The next verse continues with the positive side of what we should do: "[L]et us purify ourselves from everything that contaminates body and spirit, perfecting holiness out of reverence for God" (7:1). We must avoid both physical and spiritual pollution. We must have that reverence, or awe, for God that enables us to acquire the holiness we seek.

The description of people given in 2 Timothy 3:1-5 sounds very much like our contemporary world:

> But mark this: There will be terrible times in the last days. People will be lovers of themselves, lovers of money, boastful, proud, abusive, disobedient to their parents, ungrateful, unholy, without love, unforgiving, slanderous, without self-control, brutal, not lovers of the good, treacherous, rash, conceited, lovers of pleasure rather than lovers of God – having a form of godliness but denying its power. Have nothing to do with them.

Even if we avoid the sins listed here and thus consider ourselves good moral people, that is not enough. If we merely do the things that make it look as though we are obeying God, then we have only a "form of godliness." It is very important to have the power of godliness in our lives by purifying our hearts in obedience to God. We must also avoid associating with people who practice the things we should avoid.

These passages do not contain complete lists of things that God will not tolerate; however they highlight the kinds of things we should avoid. In most of them, sexual impurity figures prominently among the many other vices.

Although we usually think of "chaste" as referring only to sexual purity, it actually refers to the total ceremonial, moral, and religious purity that God wants in the behavior of His people. Heinrich Baltensweiler makes this point:

> The concept of purification gains however a new meaning, for the term is used to express the moral purity which is demanded in the behaviour of

Christians. Here the starting point is the fact that Christ is *hagnos*, pure, i.e. without sin (1 Jn. 3:3). Because he is pure, those who belong to him should also be pure. Through his unique sacrificial death Christ has not only made the normal sacrifices of the temple cult unnecessary, but he has also exposed their real meaning. It is a similar situation with the purity which he gives his own. It is more than ritual purity. Purity and integrity are, moreover, not merely human virtues: they indicate the relation of a person to God. Therefore this term is no longer used of sexual purity or abstinence. The NT term for that is *enkrateia*. (*The New International Dictionary of New Testament Theology*, ed. Colin Brown [Grand Rapids: Zondervan, 1978], Vol. 3, pp. 101-102)

Discussion Questions

1. Describe what a "chaste lifestyle" means to you.
2. What is the standard of purity for Christians? What, if any, does the world consider to be its standard of purity? What specifically can you, as a Christian, do about the discrepancy?
3. What are the differences among ceremonial purity, moral purity and religious purity? Why are all three necessary in your life?
4. In what areas of life do you need to be pure? How can you attain the inner purity that God commands? Which scriptures help you most?
5. What areas of impurity in your own life are the hardest for you to control? What can you do about it?
6. How is purity of heart shown in interpersonal social relationships? Business relationships? Think of a situation in which you, or someone else, might be tempted to follow a course of action that on the surface looks right but could not be done with a pure heart. How could that situation be resolved in accordance with the teachings of the Bible?
7. What is the connection between purity and holiness? Why is it important in every day life to have a pure heart,

to act from pure motives?

8. In your quest for purity in your life, what are some things you should avoid? How can you overcome the worldly influences so prevalent today?

9. Discuss the statement, "Purity of heart is to will one thing." How does this relate to integrity, commitment to God, and one's priorities?

CHAPTER 5

Who Do You Let Pull Your Strings?

"For God did not give us a spirit of timidity, but a spirit of power, of love and of self-discipline" (2 Timothy 1:7).

"I can do everything through him who gives me strength" (Philippians 4:13).

Have you ever felt like a marionette, being pulled first this way, then that way, wishing you could be the one to pull the strings? Young people feel this way sometimes. Parents are telling them one thing; the television, movies, and music lyrics are blaring out another message; their peers are pressuring them into conformity with the crowd; and other demands are confusing them. No wonder that they sometimes lash out in anger and rebel by doing things they may not really want to do.

These feelings of frustration are not limited to young people. We all feel that way sometimes. So many forces are pulling on us that we are confused. We want to take charge of our own lives, but we are distracted by too many pressures and influences. We find ourselves drifting along in the stream of humanity, not really deciding our own actions, but going along with what everyone else is doing and what others want us to do. When this happens, we may find that we are not really in charge of anything, especially our own lives.

When I was a child and wanted to do something, the excuse "Everybody else is doing it!" ensured that my parents' answer would be a firm "No." Although I was often allowed, and even encouraged, to join my friends, there had to be a better reason for wanting to do something than merely going along with the crowd. My parents did not want me thoughtlessly allowing others to pull my strings. They were trying to teach me to think for myself and make my own decisions.

We must exercise control over ourselves in order to be able to pull our own strings. If we let others pull our strings, we are letting others have control over us. If we want to decide what, or who, pulls our strings, then we must learn self-control, or self-discipline. It is up to us to decide who will be in control of our lives, what will pull our strings. To whatever we yield, that controls us.

In our world today, self-control has almost become a dirty word. We are told that we must not suppress our natural urges, we must follow our feelings no matter who else suffers. We must consider ourselves and our desires first.

"Let it all hang out!"

"Take care of Number One!"

"If it feels good, do it!"

"Our natural urges are so strong that we can't help it."

"God made me this way, and if it feels this good, it can't be wrong!"

"You only live once; have fun; don't deny yourself anything!"

These attitudes of self-indulgence are opposed to the biblical concept of self-control or self-discipline. Self-indulgence is not good for us and certainly does not bring the happiness that everyone claims to be seeking. In fact, it usually leads to even more problems.

Although often linked together, self-control is not the same as either self-denial or repression. Self-control is always good; self-denial can be either positive or negative; and repression is frequently harmful. Self-control as the Bible commands it, unlike self-denial and repression, never harms us and always benefits us.

The preceding chapter discussed being chaste, or pure. Although its meaning is often limited to sexual purity, the word really refers to purity in all of its various aspects: purity of thoughts, deeds, actions, motives, and ethics. Now we come to the concept of self-control, which usually refers to controlling our diets, our tongues, our anger, our spending habits and our will power, but not often our sexual activities. Yet, the Greek word most consistently translated "self-control" actually refers primarily to restraint in sexual matters.

It is interesting to notice how words have changed their meanings through the centuries. For example, when the King James Version of the Bible was translated, "chaste," like the Greek word it translated, had a broader meaning than merely sexual purity, which is what it means to most people today. The Greeks had a different word for controlling oneself sexually, and it is usually translated "self-control," which to us does not normally mean sexual restraint. The King James Version translates this word for controlling oneself sexually as "temperance," which in modern usage means not drinking alcoholic beverages. Yet another Greek word means being sober as opposed to being drunk, and it, too, is translated "self-control."

This may sound confusing, but it helps illustrate the value of learning what these words meant at the time the Bible was written. Such word studies are important to understanding what God really said and what it means for us today.

At least three Greek words are translated in the New Testament as "self-control," and each has a different emphasis. It will be helpful to consider the differences in meaning among them.

Enkrateia: Controlling Bodily Desires

The first word is *enkrateia* and its cognates. This is the word most consistently translated "self-control." It means having control of our bodies and our physical desires. Although it refers mainly to controlling our sexual appetites, it also includes other physical excesses. In addition it includes positive, general self-control and discipline. The root of the word has to do with having something in our power or under our control, as "gripping" something. Thus we might think of being in control of ourselves as "getting a grip on" ourselves, or "taking hold of" ourselves. It means having the strength of character to be able to control one's bodily appetites and passions.

Aristotle defined this kind of self-control by saying, "The opposite of *enkrateia* is action dominated by desire, and the man who is *enkrates* is the man who prevents desire from being the dictator of his actions and his life" (*On Virtues and Vices* 1:3). In other words, Aristotle was saying that anyone who does not have this kind of self-control allows desire or passion to pull the strings.

In the physical sense, this Greek word for self-control means to control what your body does, to control the body's various cravings. In the moral and ethical sphere, "It describes that strength of soul by which a man takes a hold of himself, takes a grip of himself, is in full control and possession of himself, so that he can restrain himself from every evil desire" (William Barclay, *Flesh and Spirit* [London: SCM Press Ltd., 1962], pp. 121-127).

Handing Control to God

However, as Christians do we really want "full control and possession" of ourselves? Surely we would rather have God in control of our lives. Yet we must exercise some control over ourselves in order to be able to surrender our strings to God for Him to pull. If we allow our strings to be pulled by desire, by passions of the moment, or by what everyone else is doing, then we do not have the capability of handing the strings over to God. We must have enough control over ourselves to take a stand and actively place ourselves under His control. God will not wrest the strings away from those we allow to control us. He does not force His will on us. We must submit to Him willingly. We make that decision for ourselves.

Romans 6:16-18 makes the point that we must decide whom we allow to control us:

> Don't you know that when you offer yourselves to someone to obey him as slaves, you are slaves to the one whom you obey – whether you are slaves to sin, which leads to death, or to obedience, which leads to righteousness? But thanks be to God that, though you used to be slaves to sin, you wholeheartedly obeyed the form of teaching to which you

were entrusted. You have been set free from sin and have become slaves to righteousness.

If we want God to control our lives, then we must offer ourselves to Him in obedience. This word for self-control, *enkrateia*, is used only seven times in six different verses in the New Testament. Perhaps one reason that it is used so seldom is that as Christians we really do not want full control of ourselves. Because of the many wonderful blessings that come to us through the grace and salvation God has given us, we should want Him to be in control. In recognition of His great love for us, we return His love by surrendering control of ourselves to Him.

Verses That Use *Enkrateia*

The meaning of self-control as sexual restraint is not obvious in most translations, but knowing this usage of the Greek word helps one understand the English. For example, Galatians 5:23 includes this word as a fruit of the Spirit. A similar list in 2 Peter 1:6 encouraging spiritual growth contains the same word. In Acts 24:25 Paul used it in speaking about faith in Jesus. The primary emphasis, but not the total meaning, of this word in all three of these passages is controlling one's sexual desires – not being dominated by passion.

In Acts 24:25 we have the account of Paul's appearance before the governor, Felix, and his wife. "As Paul discoursed on righteousness, *self-control* and the judgment to come, Felix was afraid and said, 'That's enough for now! You may leave. When I find it convenient, I will send for you.' "

Felix was married to a Jewess, so he probably knew something about Jewish teachings. Yet he lived in a society in which sexual excesses were not considered to be as wrong as they are in the Judeo-Christian context. *Enkrateia* was not a meaningless word to Felix; he must have known exactly what Paul meant.

Galatians 5:22-23 mentions a number of qualities that should be incorporated into our daily lives: "But the fruit of the Spirit is love, joy, peace, patience, kindness, goodness, faithfulness, gentleness and *self-control*." These items are in contrast to those acts of the sinful nature named in verses 19-21, several of which are related to sexual excesses.

Second Peter 1:5-9 also identifies qualities we need to develop in our lives:

> For this very reason, make every effort to add to your faith goodness; and to goodness, knowledge; and to knowledge, *self-control*; and to *self-control*, perseverance; and to perseverance, godliness; and to godliness, brotherly kindness; and to brotherly kindness, love. For if you possess these qualities in increasing measure, they will keep you from being ineffective and unproductive in your knowledge of our Lord Jesus Christ. But if anyone does not have them, he is nearsighted and blind, and has forgotten that he has been cleansed from his past sins.

Controlling one's sexual urges is an important link in the chain of qualities that enable us to be productive for the Lord.

Several virtues are common to these lists in Galatians and 2 Peter, although there are differences. Neither list is complete, but notice that control of our sexual urges is included in both. Galatians speaks of "fruit of the Spirit" and 2 Peter of "qualities" that are the result of effort on our part. Self-control in sexual matters is both a fruit of the working of God's Spirit in us and a quality that we add to our lives.

Christ has cleansed us from sin and He will help us to live as we should, but we have to make the effort to do what He wants. Grace is a free gift from God and nothing we do, not even complete obedience, can save us; but because God has saved us, we want to do the things that will please Him. God wants us to control our passions, and if He wants us to do something, He has made us capable of doing it. He gives us His Holy Spirit to aid us and make possible the attainment of the kind of life He desires for us. Thus we should try to keep these verses in our minds as goals as we try to live worthy lives.

The traits in Galatians 5 and 2 Peter 1 are characteristics of our lives, not just things we sometimes do. We need to make all of these qualities part of our whole existence. They should be the way we customarily act. However, we could conceivably act in a way that others see as godly, for example, but if it is not from the heart, if that is not really the way we are, then godliness is not a quality or fruit of our lives. These virtues define character. They are not so much what we do as what kind of people we are. Of course, the kind of people we are finds expression in the things we do.

These qualities cannot be turned on and off according to our whims. These are not things about which we can say, "Today I will choose to be kind, perhaps tomorrow I will be self-controlled." These virtues should become so much a part of us that they show others the kind of people we are and the integrity of our lives. Others will be able to see Christ living in us as we embody and exemplify these principles.

In 1 Corinthians 7:8-9, we see that sexual relations should be limited to marriage:

> Now to the unmarried and the widows I say: It is good for them to stay unmarried, as I am. But if they cannot *control themselves*, they should marry, for it is better to marry than to burn with passion.

The meaning of controlling one's sexual urges is obvious in the English translation of these verses.

First Corinthians 9:24-27 suggests that self-control is developed by constant practice, much as an athlete trains for competition:

> Do you not know that in a race all the runners run, but only one gets the prize? Run in such a way as to get the prize. Everyone who competes in the games goes into *strict training*. They do it to get a crown that will not last; but we do it to get a crown that will last forever. Therefore I do not run like a man running aimlessly; I do not fight like a man beating the air. No, I beat my body and make it my slave so that after I have preached to others, I my-self will not be disqualified for the prize.

This passage has sometimes been used to say that God wants us to practice complete sexual abstinence as well as harsh treatment of our bodies. That interpretation goes beyond what the scripture actually says. Instead, Paul compares an athletic contest, and the training for it, with the more important role of evangelism. He declares that he will make himself do whatever is necessary to be able to teach others about God.

To further illustrate the kind of self-control or "strict training" in this passage, we might think of a gymnast who has spent years training for Olympic competition. Every bodily movement must be under strict control. Think of the graceful athlete on the balance beam. Even a slight movement of an arm or a leg can be enough to change the delicate balance and cause a fall. How many times must each movement be repeated with careful muscle control before the routine is mastered! How much effort must be put into every practice session! The athlete does not literally "beat his own body," but with the sore muscles that come from such strict training, that may be a good figurative description.

In Titus 1:6-8 we find a description of the kind of person who is capable of being a leader, an elder, in the Lord's church:

> An elder must be blameless, the husband of but one wife, a man whose children believe and are not open to the charge of being wild and disobedient. Since an overseer is entrusted with God's work, he must be blameless – not overbearing, not quick-tempered, not given to much wine, not violent, not pursuing dishonest gain. Rather he must be hospitable, one who loves what is good, who is self-controlled, upright, holy and *disciplined.*

These other concepts that are associated with self-control give some further idea of what the word indicates. An elder should be someone who has a grip on himself and does not allow his strings to be pulled indiscriminately. Among other things, he should not be the kind of person who is constantly seeking someone to use for his own sexual pleasure. In other words, he must be the kind of man in whose company women are completely safe.

In these verses two different words are used that mean self-control. Each refers to a different aspect and both are important. The word that means control over one's physical desires, *enkrateia*, is translated "disciplined" in the New International Version. The other word, *sophron,* here translated "self-control," is our next consideration. Exercising self-control in one area aids in learning to control oneself in other areas.

Sophron: Controlling the Mind

This second word for self-control, *sophron* and its cognates, refers to the mental state. It means being in one's right mind, having sober judgment, being clear minded, sensible, rational, serious, reasonable; acting with propriety and prudence; being in control of one's own mind and thoughts.

The ability to control one's mental processes may not come easily, but it can be developed over time with suitable practice. Thus an older person should have more wisdom and good judgment than a younger person. A sensible person profits from experience.

As gymnasts practice, they must concentrate on what is being done. In order to learn the proper movements it is necessary to exercise the mind as well as the body. Athletes are encouraged to go through their performances mentally, picturing themselves successfully completing the complicated routines. Only a moment's lapse of concentration during a performance can spell disaster. Athletes must be mentally focused in order to make the muscles do what they have been trained to do.

Even as athletes must keep their thoughts under control, Christians are reminded in 2 Corinthians 10:5 to "take captive every thought to make it obedient to Christ." We must obey Christ not only by our actions but also in our thoughts.

Mental self-control is also urged on us in Philippians 4:8. "Finally, brothers, whatever is true, whatever is noble, whatever is right, whatever is pure, whatever is lovely, whatever is admirable – if anything is excellent or praiseworthy - think about such things." We must think about these good things rather than filling our minds with the bad things that are not in keeping with God's way.

Pure thinking on our part is encouraged in 2 Peter 3:1-2:

> Dear friends, this is now my second letter to you. I have written both of them as reminders to stimulate you to wholesome thinking. I want you to recall the words spoken in the past by the holy

prophets and the command given by our Lord and Savior through your apostles.

Reading and studying God's Word, and especially thinking about it, will help us to keep our minds under control. It takes mental exertion to keep our thoughts centered on the right things. Perhaps it takes as much effort, although in a different sphere, as it takes to keep our physical desires under control. Sometimes we are like Scarlett O'Hara in *Gone with the Wind*. We try to avoid mental effort by putting it off while saying, "I'll think about that tomorrow."

Verses That Use *Sophron*

Mark and Luke give accounts of the same incident in the life of Christ. "When they came to Jesus, they saw the man who had been possessed by the legion of demons, sitting there, dressed and in his *right mind*; and they were afraid" (Mark 5:15).

"[A]nd the people went out to see what had happened. When they came to Jesus, they found the man from whom the demons had gone out, sitting at Jesus' feet, dressed and in his *right mind*; and they were afraid" (Luke 8:35).

This man lived among the tombs and did not wear clothes. Sometimes he was chained but broke the chains. He often cut himself with rocks. After coming under the healing influence of Jesus, he was again in his right mind, able to think and behave rationally.

According to Romans 12:1-3 part of our worship to God is changing our thought patterns to be in line with His will:

> Therefore, I urge you, brothers, in view of God's mercy, to offer your bodies as living sacrifices, holy and pleasing to God – which is your spiritual worship. Do not conform any longer to the pattern of this world, but be transformed by the renewing of your mind. Then you will be able to test and approve what God's will is – his good, pleasing and perfect will.
>
> For by the grace given me I say to every one of you: Do not think of yourself more highly than you ought, but rather think of yourself with *sober judg-*

ment, in accordance with the measure of faith God
has given you.

We should not be irresponsible in the way we think, especially about ourselves. We must be aware of our limitations;
but as we learn to have more faith in God, we realize that He
will help us as we try to follow His will. Serious thoughtful-
ness is needed in order to follow the admonitions in these
verses. Time must be spent in the meditation that is necessary
for sober judgment.

In 2 Corinthians 5:11-15 Paul says that although the message of death and resurrection he preached may have seemed
irrational to his listeners, it was completely true and correct:

> Since, then, we know what it is to fear the Lord, we
> try to persuade men. What we are is plain to God,
> and I hope it is also plain to your conscience. ... If
> we are out of our mind, it is for the sake of God; if
> we are in our *right mind*, it is for you. For Christ's
> love compels us, because we are convinced that
> one died for all, and therefore all died. And he died
> for all, that those who live should no longer live
> for themselves but for him who died for them and
> was raised again.

Paul acted the way he did out of the fear of God and in order to live for Christ. He wanted to persuade everyone of
Christ's love for us and the reaction we should have because
of that love. If we are in our right minds, we will live for Christ
and not for ourselves.

Titus 2 contains instructions for various groups of Christians:
older men, older women, young women and young men.
Among other things, God insists that we be self-controlled
mentally and that we teach others to be self-controlled. If God
commands that we learn this, then it is possible to do so.

> Teach the older men to be temperate, worthy of re-
> spect, *self-controlled*, and sound in faith, in love and
> in endurance.
>
> Likewise, teach the older women to be reverent in
> the way they live, not to be slanderers or addicted

to much wine, but to teach what is good. Then they can *train* the younger women to love their husbands and children, to be *self-controlled* and pure, to be busy at home, to be kind, and to be subject to their husbands, so that no one will malign the word of God.

Similarly, encourage the young men to be *self-controlled*. In your teaching show integrity, seriousness and soundness of speech that cannot be condemned, so that those who oppose you may be ashamed because they have nothing bad to say about us. (vv. 2-8)

Our minds must be disciplined in order to be able to follow the instructions in the rest of the passage.

Disciplining Our Thoughts

A powerful verse is found in 2 Timothy 1:7. "For God did not give us a spirit of timidity, but a spirit of power, of love and of *self-discipline*." God himself gives us the strength, the power, that we need to control our thoughts, to discipline our minds. We do not have to rely solely on ourselves for the ability to pull our own strings. With power from God we can improve our abilities to keep our minds focused on the things that He wants.

Sometimes we assume that we are not able to control our thoughts, that we cannot help what comes into our minds. My mother used to say, "You can't keep the birds from flying over your head, but you can keep them from building a nest in your hair." Maybe it is not possible to keep bad thoughts from popping into our heads, but we can keep ourselves from dwelling on them. Satan introduces bad thoughts into our heads, but God gives us the power to push them out of our minds.

We often hear someone say, "Well, I'll forgive her for that, but I can't forget it!" It is easy to forget what we ought to remember, but much more difficult to forget something intentionally. The deliberate effort to forget seems to keep an idea fresh in our minds. However, with God's help we can do anything. We must make ourselves think of something else, something good, each time Satan tries to remind us of the things we ought to forget. It may be difficult to describe how to do it, but it is possible to forget something that should be put out of our minds. If we know that it can be done and that God wants us to do it, then with prayer and effort we will find the way. God will help us.

It is by the power of God that we have the ability to think and to exercise control over our minds. It is a gift of God and a blessing; one that we should appreciate and use but not abuse. We should never use our God-given mental abilities to plot evil plans.

Learning to reject that which is wrong is not only an important but also an attainable part of self-discipline.

> For the grace of God that brings salvation has appeared to all men. It teaches us to say "No" to ungodliness and worldly passions, and to live *self-controlled*, upright and godly lives in this present age, while we wait for the blessed hope – the glorious appearing of our great God and Savior, Jesus Christ, who gave himself for us to redeem us from all wickedness and to purify for himself a people that are his very own, eager to do what is good. (Titus 2:11-14)

We are defined not only by what we do but also by the things to which we say, "No." It is comforting to know that the grace of God teaches us to say, "No," to things we should not do. This is another example of the way that God helps us to discipline ourselves.

We can learn to control our minds, but we need assistance from God. If we are not pulling our own strings, whoever or whatever is doing the pulling can and will pull us away from God. We must be able to exercise some control over ourselves in order to submit to God. Only in submission to Him do we find the help we need for everything in our lives. As we learn to trust in God and Jesus, we are eager to do the right things.

Living "upright and godly lives" is another way of saying living "worthy lives."

The Discipline of Being Reasonable

Paul was in prison because of his teachings about Jesus. In his defense before Festus, he related the important facts of his life both before and after his vision of Christ on the road to Damascus. When Paul spoke of the death and resurrection of Christ, Festus accused him of being out of his mind, driven mad by his great learning. Paul's response to this charge is in Acts 26:25. " 'I am not insane, most excellent Festus,' Paul replied. 'What I am saying is true and *reasonable.*' " Although some individuals consider that the Good News about Christ is unreasonable, it is indeed the true message from God, which should be accepted by all rational minds.

Two passages in 1 Timothy discuss women's activities and both include the idea of reasonableness. First Timothy 2:9-10 shows that good deeds are more important than fancy clothes. "I also want women to dress modestly, with decency and *propriety*, not with braided hair or gold or pearls or expensive clothes, but with good deeds, appropriate for women who profess to worship God." Propriety includes acting with good sense and moderation.

The second passage is 1 Timothy 2:15. "But women will be kept safe through childbirth – if they continue in faith, love and holiness with *propriety*." Acting with propriety corresponds to the idea of living worthily or doing activities that are appropriate for those who worship God.

First Timothy 3:2 contains part of a description of the kind of person who is qualified to lead God's people. "Now the overseer must be above reproach, the husband of but one wife, temperate, *self-controlled*, respectable, hospitable, able to teach."

A parallel passage is in Titus 1:8. "Rather he must be hospitable, one who loves what is good, who is *self-controlled*, upright, holy and disciplined."

Leaders of the church must be reasonable, rational, sensible, prudent and in control of themselves and their thoughts. They must also be temperate and disciplined, as we see from the use of the other two Greek words meaning self-control.

Another verse that uses more than one of these words is 1 Peter 4:7, which gives a compelling reason for controlling ourselves and our minds. "[B]e *clear minded* and self-controlled so that you can pray." Without clear-minded control of ourselves, we will not spend the time we should in prayer. Instead we will let other things pull us away from talking with God.

The importance of understanding the differences in meanings among these three words is demonstrated by verses that contain more than one Greek word for self-discipline. *Sophron* is translated in 1 Peter 4:7 as "clear minded" and the word translated "self-controlled" is the next one in our study.

Nepho: Self-Restraint

The third word for "self-control," *nepho* and its cognates, means the opposite of intoxication. It is thus sometimes translated "temperance." It refers to sobriety, either literally or figuratively. Literally, it means to abstain from intoxicating drink. Figuratively, it means to be free from every form of mental and spiritual drunkenness – free from excess, passion, rashness and confusion; to be well-balanced, self-possessed under all circumstances; to exercise self-restraint or self-control for one's own good.

Although the literal sense is often implied, in the New Testament the figurative sense is prominent. This kind of temperance, or self-control, refers to mental alertness, clarity of mind, appropriate frame of mind, and the good judgment that results.

Certainly one must control himself or herself in relation to intoxicating drink and other drugs. But one must also be careful not to become intoxicated by money, work, power, sports, recreation, the pursuit of success, beauty, intelligence or anything else that can pull us away from God.

Verses That Use *Nepho*

This word for self-control is used in the New Testament to refer to the temperate lifestyle required of bishops or overseers (1 Timothy 3:2), women (1 Timothy 3:11), and elders (Titus 2:2). The main point seems to be the self-control necessary for effective ministry. It is important to keep a balance in our lives: not to be dominated by any one thing, but to consider carefully and thoughtfully all aspects of a situation.

In the description of one who is capable of leading God's people, 1 Timothy 3:2 uses two different words for "self-control," thus indicating different aspects of the subject. "Now the overseer must be above reproach, the husband of but one wife, *temperate*, self-controlled, respectable, hospitable, able to teach." Not only must the overseer be sober in his activities but he also must be mentally disciplined, exercising good judgment.

First Timothy 3:11 points out that it is important for Christian women likewise to show sobriety in their lives. "In the same way, their wives are to be women worthy of respect, not malicious talkers but *temperate* and trustworthy in everything."

Another verse that uses two different words for self-control is Titus 2:2. "Teach the older men to be *temperate*, worthy of respect, self-controlled, and sound in faith, in love and in endurance." These Christian men must not engage in any kind of intoxicating activities, and they must use sound judgment in all areas.

Sobriety

Both the literal and figurative meanings of this word are included in 1 Thessalonians 5:6-8:

> So then, let us not be like others, who are asleep, but let us be alert and *self-controlled*. For those who sleep, sleep at night, and those who get drunk, get drunk at night. But since we belong to the day, let us be *self-controlled*, putting on faith and love as a breastplate, and the hope of salvation as a helmet.

Paul contrasts self-control and drunkenness, but he does not limit the meaning to actual drunkenness from alcoholic beverages. He also speaks figuratively, as is shown by the inclusion of faith, love and hope.

Sober thinking is also required in 2 Timothy 4:5. "But you, *keep your head* in all situations, endure hardship, do the work of an evangelist, discharge all the duties of your ministry." If one is intemperate in any way, it is impossible to perform the duties pleasing to God.

Three passages in 1 Peter show the necessity of clear thinking in order to be prepared for what the future holds for us. Each of these verses ties our self-control to our relationship to God: we imitate His holiness, we pray to Him, and we stand firm in our faith in Him.

First Peter 1:13 alludes to the other kinds of self-control while requiring sobriety:

> Therefore, prepare your minds for action; be *self-controlled*; set your hope fully on the grace to be given you when Jesus Christ is revealed. As obedient children, do not conform to the evil desires you had when you lived in ignorance. But just as he who called you is holy, so be holy in all you do; for it is written: "Be holy, because I am holy."

If we prepare our minds, we exercise mental self-control; if we resist evil desires, we exercise physical self-control. Again we see the importance of being pure and holy in everything.

First Peter 4:7 shows that we cannot pray properly when our minds are clouded by intemperate behavior. "The end of all things is near. Therefore be clear minded and *self-controlled* so that you can pray."

Knowing that we are not alone in being plagued by the devil will help give us the courage to stand up for what is right. First Peter 5:8-9 says:

> Be *self-controlled* and alert. Your enemy the devil prowls around like a roaring lion looking for someone to devour. Resist him, standing firm in the faith, because you know that your brothers throughout the world are undergoing the same kind of sufferings.

It takes both sober thinking and being aware of what is happening for us to resist the evil that is in the world.

These verses plainly show that we need God in our lives in order to control ourselves. We also see the importance of prayer and relying on God's grace.

To have this kind of self-control, or temperance, we must avoid impairing our minds with alcohol, other drugs or anything else that will interfere with our being sober minded, alert and self-controlled. We may not be able to control ourselves while we are under the influence of intoxicating substances, but we can control whether or not we put these mind-altering chemicals into our bodies.

We must be aware of all aspects of self-control in order to prevent the devil from pulling our strings. God will help us, but we must do all we can to be ready and able to resist the devil.

What the World Thinks of Self-Control

The devil wants us to think he is no longer active today. That way he can slip up on us without our being alarmed. However, evil is certainly in the world today, and we must be on our guard. Many voices around us are saying things about self-control that are not true. Many of these voices are so subtle that their influence is not easily recognized. We need to be aware of these forces and learn to distinguish right from wrong. We must learn to control ourselves before we make mistakes that change our lives forever.

Messages from the Media

Radio, television, movies, song lyrics and newspapers are constantly blaring out messages opposed to the standards set in the Bible. When we accept these messages, we are exchanging the truth of God for a lie. Self-control as it is taught in the Bible is good, but the world today tells us that it is bad.

As we look around, we see evidence that many individuals are making desire the dictator of their actions. Desire, especially sexual desire, seems to be the dominant motivation in today's society. Fulfilling that desire without reserve is depicted as the ideal. Society seems to be telling our young people that the sexual urge is the most important area of their lives. Sexuality is important, but it should never be the most important part of anyone's life.

Nor should the most important part of our lives be the desire to have the most fashionable clothes, the fanciest and fastest car, the best house to live in, the highest salary possible, etc. We certainly should do our best in all legitimate endeavors, but if any one thing becomes the consuming force in our lives, we need to be careful. There is something much more important than success or creature comforts. We need to exercise self-control in order to keep these desires from pulling us away from God and the more important spiritual side of our lives.

When we see all around us the way passions seem to control everything and everyone, we sometimes feel that nothing can be done – it is just too strong for us. But is that true? Remember, self-control is a command of God. Because it is commanded, we can be assured that we are able to obey. God gave us these strong sexual urges, therefore there is nothing wrong with them. Sexual intercourse as God intended it is good, pure and a beautiful expression of love between husband and wife. It is the misuse of our sexual urges that is condemned and must be controlled. We all need to realize that sexual urges are wonderful in their proper place and that it really is worthwhile as well as possible to remain virgins until marriage.

The worldly view seems to be: "Sex is such a powerful drive that I can't control it even if I want to, so why should I try?" From all sides we hear there is nothing wrong with enjoying our sexuality to the fullest: anytime, anywhere and with anyone; it is the normal thing to do.

In some cases, parents say about their children, "I know they won't avoid sexual encounters, so I'll just try to prepare them for it and make sure they are careful. I'll make sure they practice safe sex."

On a recent TV talk show parents and their children were discussing teenage sexual activities. Most of the parents said that they knew their children would not wait until marriage to have sexual intercourse so they would rather they "did it" at home where it would be "safer."

Even among Christians the feeling sometimes is: "God made me with this strong sex drive, so He must have intended for me to use it without limits; otherwise, why would He have made it feel so good? He made me this way; I can't help it."

All of this is trying to say we are unable to pull our own strings, that we have no control over ourselves; passion and desire are so strong that they will pull our strings and there is nothing we can do about it. But is that true?

Are These Arguments Valid?

To determine if these arguments are valid, we must look in the Bible. Some individuals say that God made us this way, so it is His fault, not ours, if we cannot remain sexually pure until marriage. This argument is made by both heterosexuals and homosexuals, but it is not valid for anyone, as we can see from studying the following passages.

James 1:13-15 makes it clear that we cannot blame God for our temptations or for our giving in to those temptations:

> When tempted, no one should say, "God is tempting me." For God cannot be tempted by evil, nor does he tempt anyone; but each one is tempted when, by his own evil desire, he is dragged away and enticed. Then, after desire has conceived, it gives birth to sin; and sin, when it is full-grown, gives birth to death.

If we surrender to temptation, it is our own fault, not God's. First John 2:15-17 also makes it plain that temptation to do evil does not come from God:

> Do not love the world or anything in the world. If anyone loves the world, the love of the Father is not in him. For everything in the world – the cravings of sinful man, the lust of his eyes and the boasting of what he has and does – comes not from the Father but from the world. The world and its desires pass away, but the man who does the will of God lives forever.

If we love God and thus try to please Him, we will be better off than those who love the world.

Our sexuality is a God-given blessing, but He did not intend for us to misuse it.

> The body is not meant for sexual immorality, but for the Lord, and the Lord for the body. By his power God raised the Lord from the dead, and he will raise us also. Do you not know that your bodies are members of Christ himself? Shall I then take the members of Christ and unite them with a prosti-

tute? Never! Do you not know that he who unites himself with a prostitute is one with her in body? For it is said, "The two will become one flesh." But he who unites himself with the Lord is one with him in spirit.

Flee from sexual immorality. All other sins a man commits are outside his body, but he who sins sexually sins against his own body. Do you not know that your body is a temple of the Holy Spirit, who is in you, whom you have received from God? You are not your own; you were bought at a price. Therefore honor God with your body. (1 Corinthians 6:13-20)

God does not force self-control on us just as He does not force obedience on us. If we give in to lust, it is our fault, not His, and we are the ones who suffer the consequences. When we turn away from God, He allows it; He does not force us to let Him to pull our strings.

Sexual Perversions

Romans 1:18-32 refers to those who should have plainly seen the nature of God, but who turned away from Him to do their own foolish sins:

The wrath of God is being revealed from heaven against all the godlessness and wickedness of men who suppress the truth by their wickedness, since what may be known about God is plain to them, because God has made it plain to them. For since the creation of the world God's invisible qualities – his eternal power and divine nature – have been clearly seen, being understood from what has been made, so that men are without excuse.

For although they knew God, they neither glorified him as God nor gave thanks to him, but their thinking became futile and their foolish hearts were darkened. Although they claimed to be wise, they became fools and exchanged the glory of the immortal God for images made to look like mortal man and birds and animals and reptiles.

Therefore God gave them over in the sinful desires of their hearts to sexual impurity for the de-
grading of their bodies with one another. They exchanged the truth of God for a lie, and worshiped
and served created things rather than the Creator
– who is forever praised. Amen.
Because of this, God gave them over to shameful
lusts. Even their women exchanged natural relations for unnatural ones. In the same way the men
also abandoned natural relations with women and
were inflamed with lust for one another. Men committed indecent acts with other men, and received
in themselves the due penalty for their pervision.
Furthermore, since they did not think it worthwhile to retain the knowledge of God, he gave them
over to a depraved mind, to do what ought not to
be done. They have become filled with every kind
of wickedness, evil, greed and depravity. They are
full of envy, murder, strife, deceit and malice. They
are gossips, slanderers, God-haters, insolent, arro-
gant and boastful; they invent ways of doing evil;
they disobey their parents; they are senseless, faith-
less, heartless, ruthless. Although they know God's
righteous decree that those who do such things deserve death, they not only continue to do these very
things but also approve of those who practice them.

Some individuals say these verses are condemning only the
idolatrous sexual activities in connection with the pagan tem-
ples but are not condemning "normal" loving, committed homosexual relationships. However, these verses are not saying, "These acts are wrong because they are done in the service of an idol." Rather, they are saying, "Worship to an idol
is so bad that it causes people to do these despicable acts!"
God condemns both idolatry and homosexual activities.

Homosexuality is only one sexual perversion condemned
by God. He also condemns adultery and other wrongful sexual relationships. Leviticus 18 is very explicit in what constitutes sexual perversions. God forbids sexual relations with:
mother, step-mother, sister, grandchild, step-sister, aunt,

daughter-in-law, sister-in-law, a woman and her daughter or granddaughter, a neighbor's wife, or another man. Leviticus 20:13 plainly states, "If a man lies with a man as one lies with a woman, both of them have done what is detestable. They must be put to death; their blood will be on their own heads."

Sexual perversions are also condemned in the New Testament. God is no more pleased with adultery, which our society seems to have accepted, than He is with homosexual activities, which our society seems to be on the brink of accepting. The same scriptures that condemn one condemn the other (Galatians 5:19-21; Revelation 21:8).

In 1 Corinthians 7:3-5 God also condemns arbitrary abstinence between husband and wife:

> The husband should fulfill his marital duty to his wife, and likewise the wife to her husband. The wife's body does not belong to her alone but also to her husband. In the same way, the husband's body does not belong to him alone but also to his wife. Do not deprive each other except by mutual consent and for a time, so that you may devote yourselves to prayer. Then come together again so that Satan will not tempt you because of your lack of self-control.

Even those professing to be good Christians sometimes overlook this command. God intended for husbands and wives to enjoy each other's bodies. It is not right for one spouse to use his or her sexuality to manipulate or punish the other. Nor is the husband given the right to force himself on his wife against her will. Colossians 3:19 is clear about this: "Husbands, love your wives and do not be harsh with them."

Some individuals seem to think humans have no more control over their passions than an animal in heat. However, God has made us more capable than that, and we deserve more respect than being compared to animals in this way.

Many individuals want to do what is right. Those who exercise the self-control necessary to resist such strong temptations need to be helped and encouraged. They need to know that it is good to remain virgins until they marry. Both sexes need to know that virginity is a beautiful gift that can be given only once. Once it is given, it can never be regained.

Although something precious is lost forever when a person, either male or female, loses his or her virginity, that is no excuse to quit trying to live up to God's ideal. God can and will forgive us, but it is up to us to continue to act the way He wants us to act. Even if someone has made a mistake, he or she can be forgiven and then remain pure from that time on.

"Safe Sex?"

We are told it is important to practice "safe sex." But is there such a thing as safe sex? No more so than there is such a thing as a safe game of Russian roulette. Participating in unprotected sexual intercourse is like putting five bullets into a revolver, spinning the chamber, pointing the six-shooter at your head and pulling the trigger. You may not be killed, but you probably will be. So-called "safe sex" can be compared to putting only one bullet into the chamber – the odds are a lot better, but you may still be in trouble. No kind of protection is 100 percent safe against either pregnancy or sexually transmitted diseases. It is essential to realize that fact before it becomes too late.

The only safe sex is to abstain from sexual relations until a marriage in which both partners are virgins, then for each to remain faithful to that one spouse for life. That is the way God planned it, and that is the only way to gain the fullest and deepest satisfaction and enjoyment from a sexual relationship.

Sexual fulfillment apart from marriage is presented to us every day as the normal lifestyle. That is why it is so important for us to keep in sight God's ideal of what He wants for us and what He knows is best for us. We know that by God's grace we are capable of following His will and that His good and perfect will is always in our best interests.

How Can We Resist Temptation?

So many temptations are trying to pull our strings that we need help in knowing how to resist. Fortunately the Bible gives us guidance in this area as in many others.

> Let us behave decently, as in the daytime, not in orgies and drunkenness, not in sexual immorality and

debauchery, not in dissension and jealousy. Rather,
clothe yourselves with the Lord Jesus Christ, and
do not think about how to gratify the desires of the
sinful nature. (Romans 13:13-14)

If we spend our time thinking about gratifying our bodily
desires, we will not have time to think about Jesus and the
things He wants us to do.

We should get as far away from temptation as possible.

Flee from sexual immorality. All other sins a man
commits are outside his body, but he who sins sexually sins against his own body. Do you not know
that your body is a temple of the Holy Spirit, who is
in you, whom you have received from God? You are
not your own; you were bought at a price. Therefore
honor God with your body. (1 Corinthians 6:18-20)

Do not put yourself in a compromising situation.
Remember, your body should be used to honor God, not to
gratify sinful desires.

The Bible gives us many examples of right and wrong behavior. God wants us to see what happened to people in the
past who disobeyed Him so that we will learn the wisdom of
following His ways. In 1 Corinthians 10:1-13 we find a reference to the Israelites during their wilderness wanderings:

For I do not want you to be ignorant of the fact,
brothers, that our forefathers were all under the
cloud and that they all passed through the sea. ...
God was not pleased with most of them; their bodies were scattered over the desert.

Now these things occurred as examples, to keep
us from setting our hearts on evil things as they did.
... We should not commit sexual immorality, as
some of them did. ...

These things happened to them as examples and
were written down as warnings for us, on whom
the fulfillment of the ages has come. So, if you think
you are standing firm, be careful that you don't fall!
No temptation has seized you except what is common to man. And God is faithful; he will not let you

be tempted beyond what you can bear. But when
you are tempted, he will also provide a way out so
that you can stand up under it.

We can look at the examples of others, especially those in
the Old Testament, to help us do what is right. God has
promised that there will be a way out of temptation for us;
no temptation will be impossible for us to resist.

One of the best ways to resist temptation is to pray to God
for help. Another way is to plan ahead what we will do in
a given situation. This planning ahead involves the second
word for self-control that we discussed – *sophron*, or mental
concentration. If we make up our minds ahead of time what
is right and what is wrong, we will be better able to stand
up for the right.

Part of planning ahead is studying the Scriptures, and studying the Scriptures helps us not to sin. Psalm 119:11 shows the
importance of knowing God's Word so well that it becomes
a part of us. "I have hidden your word in my heart that I
might not sin against you."

Realizing the importance of controlling ourselves sexually
is yet another way of enabling ourselves to resist temptations.

In 1 Thessalonians 4:1-8, we see again that we should follow God's will for our lives:

> Finally, brothers, we instructed you how to live in
> order to please God, as in fact you are living. Now
> we ask you and urge you in the Lord Jesus to do
> this more and more. You know what instructions
> we gave you by the authority of the Lord Jesus.
>
> It is God's will that you should be holy; that you
> should avoid sexual immorality; that each of you
> should learn to control his own body in a way that
> is holy and honorable, not in passionate lust like
> the heathen, who do not know God. ... The Lord
> will punish men for all such sins, as we have al-
> ready told you and warned you. For God did not
> call us to be impure, but to live a holy life. Therefore,
> he who rejects this instruction does not reject man
> but God, who gives you his Holy Spirit.

God wants us to be pure and holy. He wants us to be honorable. We should want to please Him because of all the blessings He has given to us. Our lives will be much happier if we follow His will for us.

Self-control is something we are capable of learning, otherwise God would not have told us to learn to control our own bodies. Perhaps we cannot stop the desire from being there, but we can control ourselves and refrain from acting in a sinful way. We can, with God's help, pull our own strings. We must say "No!" to anything that would pull us away from God.

Why Resist?

When I was a teenager, we were told that the sex drive is the strongest human craving. The reason we were told this was to make us aware that we must work hard to resist that drive. However, the message that seems to have come through is, "It's too strong for us. We can't resist. We can't help ourselves."

We were also told that we should avoid premarital sexual relations because of the possibility of pregnancy or sexually transmitted diseases. But then along came The Pill, and girls thought they did not have to worry about getting pregnant. Also, there was penicillin, so the threat of disease was no longer such an important deterrent.

We were short-changed. We were given bad information. We were not given the real reason for controlling ourselves sexually. We should have been told, "That's what God wants, and what He wants you to do is always what is best for you."

We can give many reasons for abstaining from sexual relations until marriage, but for Christians the crucial argument is that it is a command of God. The current talk about "safe sex" seems to be motivated more by fear of AIDS than by fear of God. When a cure for AIDS is found, then yet another deterrent will disappear. The bottom line must still be: we want to obey God because that is what He wants, and that is what is best for us in every way.

It is true that God made us with strong sexual drives. That is part of his divine will – "his good, pleasing and perfect will" (Romans 12:2). Used in the right way, sex is a beautiful expression of love; it is good and pure and right. God wants us to be happy, and He knows what will make us happy. He knows because He is the One who made us the way we are. Because He wants us to be happy, He has set limits on sexual activities, even as He has set limits on other things that we do. It is not that He wants to keep us from having fun, but He wants what will be best for us in the long run. Instant gratification is not enough for a lifetime of happiness.

There is nothing wrong with sexual urges nor is there anything wrong with sexual intercourse. It is only when we abuse this wonderful, beautiful gift from God that we get into trouble. It is the misuse that is wrong and brings unhappiness to us. We must exercise self-control in this area as in many others. Only when we use this God-given blessing in keeping with God's instructions will we find the truest and purest happiness.

The fact that God has given us a beautiful gift does not mean we have the right to use that gift indiscriminately. Perhaps we can understand this principle better if we consider something else God has given us that we must limit. The ability to speak is truly a marvelous gift from God. Yet, being able to talk does not mean that we never need to control our speech. James 1:26 makes clear the need to use restraint in our speech. "If anyone considers himself religious and yet does not keep a tight rein on his tongue, he deceives himself and his religion is worthless."

Control of one's sexuality is only one aspect of self-control that needs to be considered. More attention has been given in this chapter to the kind of self-control described by the Greek word *enkrateia* because its lack is so conspicuous in our society today. This is an important area in which we need to learn the difference between right and wrong. The world is constantly giving wrong information, and it is up to concerned Christians to speak up for biblical teachings. We need to know how to live worthy lives in spite of what confronts us.

What Is at Stake?

Romans 8:6-9 shows us why handing our strings over to God for Him to pull is so important:

> If a person's thinking is controlled by his sinful self, then there is spiritual death. But if a person's thinking is controlled by the Spirit, then there is

life and peace. Why is this true? Because if a person's thinking is controlled by his sinful self, then that person is against God. That person refuses to obey God's law. And really that person is not able to obey God's law. Those people who are ruled by their sinful selves cannot please God. But you are not ruled by your sinful selves. You are ruled by the Spirit, if that Spirit of God really lives in you. (EASY-TO-READ VERSION)

We do not want the spiritual death that is the end of those who are controlled by their own sins. We want the life and peace that is promised to those who obey God's laws. We want to please God, and we want His spirit to live within us. By controlling our physical cravings and our mental processes and by keeping a sensible balance in our lives, we should have enough control over ourselves to allow God to pull our strings. The purpose of controlling ourselves is to make us better able to live our lives worthily in His service.

First John 3:7-10 draws a sharp distinction between righteousness and sinfulness:

Dear children, do not let anyone lead you astray. He who does what is right is righteous, just as he is righteous. He who does what is sinful is of the devil, because the devil has been sinning from the beginning. The reason the Son of God appeared was to destroy the devil's work. No one who is born of God will continue to sin, because God's seed remains in him; he cannot go on sinning, because he has been born of God. This is how we know who the children of God are and who the children of the devil are: Anyone who does not do what is right is not a child of God; neither is anyone who does not love his brother.

The aim of self-control is positive, not negative. We do not hurt ourselves when we try to keep from being dominated by our passions, when we try to keep our minds clear and pure, and when we try to think and act soberly and with good judgment.

We might oversimplify the meaning of self-control and say that it means having the good sense to do what we should do and not to do what we should not do. Or, as Isaiah 1:16-17 says: "Stop doing wrong, learn to do right!"

Discussion Questions

1. Why do you think self-control is so important in the Bible? Why do you think the idea of self-control has become unpopular in today's world?
2. How does your relationship to God affect your ability to control yourself?
3. How do you correlate the ideas of self-control and of being under God's control? What does it mean to you to "let God pull your strings"? How can you turn your strings over to Him to pull? Think of some time in your own life when you turned yourself over to God. How did you do it?
4. How would you explain the differences among the kinds of self-control discussed in this chapter? How are each of these aspects of self-control important in your life?
5. Think of some time that you have forgiven someone and you really wanted to forgive and forget. What did you do to forget the hurt and resentment you originally felt against that person?
6. What are some areas of your life in which you need to exercise more self-control? What specific steps can you take to gain more control over yourself in these areas?
7. What messages do you hear coming from the media (movies, song lyrics, newspapers, television, etc.) that contradict the biblical messages of self-control? How can you overcome these worldly influences? What are some ways that you can resist the temptations that are so common today?
8. What can you do to help individuals, especially teens and other young adults, resist the temptation to give in to their sexual desires? How can you convince someone of the importance of virginity while still showing the beauty and sanctity of one's God-given sexuality?
9. Why is the slogan "Practice Safe Sex" inadequate?

CHAPTER 6

𝒜 Faith-Full Christian

"You need to persevere so that when you have done the will of God, you will receive what he has promised" (Hebrews 10:36).

When someone says, "That person is a faithful Christian," what comes first to your mind? Does it indicate merely that the person is at church every time the doors are open? Does it imply only that the person is known as having good moral character? Or does it have a deeper significance? If routine attendance and good morals are not the whole criteria, then what is a faithful Christian? What does it mean to be faithful?

To answer these questions we need to explore the meanings of both "faith" and "faithful."

Three Aspects of Faith

The word "faith" is used in the New Testament in at least three ways.

1. The Faith. This meaning of faith refers to the facts of the gospel that must be believed in order to be followers of the one true God. It is the body of information about Jesus and God revealed in the Bible. Jude 3 uses "the faith" in this objective sense: "I felt I had to write and urge you to contend for *the faith* that was once for all entrusted to the saints." The faith was what had been taught about Jesus. False teachers were trying to deny the sovereignty and lordship of Jesus Christ.

Jude reminded the Christians of some of the things the Lord had done throughout history and urged them to stand up for what they knew to be true.

The apostle Paul learned the truths of the gospel directly from Jesus Christ. "[T]he gospel I preached is not something that man made up. I did not receive it from any man, nor was I taught it; rather, I received it by revelation from Jesus Christ" (Galatians 1:11-12). Before being confronted by Jesus, Paul had been persecuting Christians. After Paul learned the truth, he began preaching it. Some of the churches in Judea did not know him personally but had heard about him. The report they received was that "The man who formerly persecuted us is now preaching *the faith* he once tried to destroy" (v. 23). Paul was proclaiming the information that he had obtained from Jesus Himself, the same facts of the gospel that Paul had once denied and fought against.

This aspect of faith is WHAT we believe.

2. Belief. A second meaning of faith is believing in the faith, accepting as true the body of information presented in the Bible as the words of God, comprehending that God exists, giving intellectual agreement or assent to what the Bible says.

In James 2:19 we see that even the demons have this kind of faith. "You *believe* that there is one God. Good! Even the demons *believe* that – and shudder."

The demons are aware that there is one God, but they only tremble in fear at the thought, doing nothing to change the way they act or what they are. However, merely accepting these things as true is not enough. God expects us to act on that faith.

> What good is it, my brothers, if a man claims to have *faith* but has no deeds? Can such *faith* save him? Suppose a brother or sister is without clothes and daily food. If one of you says to him, "Go, I wish you well; keep warm and well fed," but does nothing about his physical needs, what good is it?" In the same way, *faith* by itself, if it is not accompanied by action, is dead.
>
> But someone will say, "You have *faith*; I have deeds."

> Show me your *faith* without deeds, and I will
> show you my *faith* by what I do. (James 2:14-18)

This second aspect of faith is THAT we believe the gospel is true, whether we act on our belief or not.

3. Trust. A third meaning of faith is trust. Intellectual acceptance of the facts revealed to us about God and what He has done for us throughout history is the first step in trusting Him. When we believe the things we learn about God, we know that He is trustworthy, that He is able to do what He says He will do. The more we learn about God, the more we realize that we can trust Him, that we can rely on His promises.

When a stranger tells us something, we generally accept or reject what is said on the basis of the message rather than the messenger, because we do not have the experience to know if that person is reliable. However, when a trusted friend tells us something, we may readily accept the message because we trust the messenger. Our belief in the message is then not only based on the message itself but to a great extent is also based on our personal knowledge of our friend's integrity.

Jesus was God's messenger to us. We know we can trust Him because we have learned that He is trustworthy and reliable. We can have faith in Him as a personal friend. We trust Him because we know Him and know that He is able to do everything He has said He will do. This trust is a personal relationship, a dependence on His love and care. If we truly believe in both God and Jesus, we must live by that faith. Living by faith involves acting on our faith, hoping to go to heaven, obeying what God says, and committing our lives to Him.

This aspect of faith is WHOM we believe. This is such an important facet of faith that it demands more attention. It includes and builds on the other two meanings.

Pistis: Faith as Trust

The Greek word translated as both "faith" and "faithful" is *pistis*. Liddel-Scott's *Greek-English Lexicon* lists the first meaning of this word as "trust in others, faith." Then follows a long list of related meanings with the ideas of confidence, assurance, reliability and trust being prominent. The main emphasis of the Greek word is that if we have faith in something, we have confidence in the truth of that which we believe. If we have faith in a person, we are sure that person is trustworthy. It is more than merely supposing or wishing something to be true. The verb form, *pisteuo*, means to "trust, put faith in, rely on" a person, thing or statement.

If we have *pistis* in something or someone, we can be sure of it even if we cannot see it. We have faith that the sun will rise tomorrow even though the clouds may obscure our view of it. We even know what time to expect it. It is not just that we assume intellectually that it will happen, but that we rely on its happening to such an extent that we plan our lives around our belief that the sun will rise tomorrow. We can have this conviction because that is what the sun has always done in the past; it has always faithfully run its promised course. We have not experienced tomorrow's sunrise, we cannot prove by our five senses that it will rise, but we have faith that it will happen.

In his *Essays in Biblical Greek* (Oxford 1889, p. 87), Edwin Hatch says that *pistis*

> is not used of a vague and mystical sentiment, the hazy state of mind which precedes knowledge, like a nebula which has not yet taken a definite outline or become condensed into a star, but that it is a state of firm mental conviction, based upon a certain conception of the nature of God; hence it is used in close connexion [sic.] with the strongest word for full assurance, viz. *plerophoreisthai* Romans 4:20, 21 "He waxed strong through faith, giving glory to God, and being fully assured that what He had promised He is able also to perform."

As we study some verses that use *pistis* we should gain a clearer understanding of the meaning. In some of our other word studies we have been able to look at all the verses in the New Testament that use that particular word. However, *pistis* is such a common word that we cannot look at every instance of its use in the New Testament. Hence we shall select only a few passages that will help our understanding. The words in italics are translations of *pistis* and its cognates.

Trusting God

We can learn some important things about faith from Romans 4. Verse 3 quotes from Genesis 15:6: "What does the Scripture say? 'Abraham *believed* God, and it was credited to him as righteousness.' "

Abraham did not do the works of the Law of Moses to earn this righteousness. Indeed he could not even try, because he lived long before the Law of Moses was given on Mount Sinai. Rather he trusted God, as we see in verses 4-5:

> Now when a man works, his wages are not credited to him as a gift, but as an obligation. However, to the man who does not work but *trusts* God who justifies the wicked, his *faith* is credited as righteousness.

When a person has a job, the employer owes that person a salary. But when we are "working" for God, there is nothing that we can do that will obligate Him to "pay" us with salvation or grace or righteousness or anything else. God gives to us freely, because He loves us, not because we have worked to earn His gifts.

Verses 9-12 show that Abraham's faith came before circumcision, thus allowing people other than Jews to be considered righteous because of their faith in God. Abraham is the father of all who believe, even though they may not be his children in the flesh. Verses 13-15 continue to show that it was not by obeying the Law of Moses that righteousness came, but by faith in God.

The promise of grace belongs to all of Abraham's descendants, whether by faith or by flesh, as is shown in verses 16-17. Abraham is the father of the faithful.

Verse 17 says something important about the nature of God. "[Abraham] is our father in the sight of God, in whom he *believed* – the God who gives life to the dead."

While Abraham and Sarah were still childless, God told Abraham he would have many descendants. Abraham knew that he and his wife were both so elderly that their reproductive life was dead, yet he knew that God gives life to the dead. Although he did not understand how God was going to do this, he was convinced that God could and would allow him to have children. Abraham believed that God could do what He promised. Romans 4:18-22 explains and defines that faith:

> Against all hope, Abraham in hope *believed* and so became the father of many nations, just as it had been said to him, "So shall your offspring be." Without weakening in his *faith*, he faced the fact that his body was as good as dead – since he was about a hundred years old – and that Sarah's womb was also dead. Yet he did not waver through unbelief regarding the promise of God, but was strengthened in his *faith* and gave glory to God, being fully persuaded that God had power to do what he had promised. This is why "it was credited to him as righteousness."

We learn from Genesis 17:17 and 18:12 that Abraham as well as Sarah laughed at the promise of a son. Yet there is no mention in Romans of what we might consider a lapse of faith on his part. Although Abraham could not understand how a 100-year-old man and a 90-year-old woman could have a baby, he accepted it. By human standards, this was impossible; his knowledge of normal reproduction told him there was no hope that this could happen. Yet he believed that God's promises were more sure to be kept than even the laws of nature. Here we have an important indication of the source and basis of biblical faith (in contrast to non-biblical understandings of "faith"): it is derived from the word and promises of God. To Abraham's credit, he did not waver in his trust in God. His faith was strengthened, and he gave the glory to God, knowing that God was able to give life to the dead and to keep any and all promises He made. It is all right to lack understanding of how God will do something as long as we trust that He is able to do what He says He will do.

Romans 4:20 tells us that Abraham was strengthened in his faith and gave glory to God. One way to strengthen our faith is to recognize God's activities in our lives. The more we are aware of the blessings He gives us, the greater our faith in Him will be. And the more we praise and glorify God, the more we are aware of His gifts to us; the more we are aware, the more we will praise Him, and the greater our faith will be.

Abraham could not honor God by giving Him perfect obedience, and neither can we. However, Abraham did glorify God by being absolutely confident that God would do what He said, even though it seemed impossible. It was this act of faith, this way of honoring God by trusting Him that was credited to Abraham as righteousness. Abraham was "fully persuaded" concerning God's word – His promises and power. That is the nature of biblical, saving faith: to be completely convinced concerning what God says and to act accordingly.

Romans 4:23-25 assures us that we, too, can be credited with righteousness the same as Abraham:

> The words "it was credited to him" were written not for him alone, but also for us, to whom God will credit righteousness – for us who *believe* in him who raised Jesus our Lord from the dead. He was delivered over to death for our sins and was raised to life for our justification.

Christians believe that God gives life to the dead. We believe God raised Jesus from the dead. When we accept as fact that God could and did resurrect Jesus, our belief in God increases, and it is credited to us as righteousness. We trust Him to do what He says He will do, and that faith becomes central to our existence. We know Him, we know what He has done for us, and we know He will continue to bless us.

Paul expressed this same confidence in 2 Timothy 1:11-12:

> And of this gospel I was appointed a herald and an apostle and a teacher. That is why I am suffering as I am. Yet I am not ashamed, because I know whom I have *believed*, and am convinced that he is able to guard what I have entrusted to him for that day.

Paul trusted God because he knew Him so intimately that he was convinced of His power. Paul knew that although he was being persecuted, God was still with him and cared for him. He knew that with God's help he would eventually triumph. He knew he could trust God.

This kind of faith is summed up on a bumper sticker that was popular some years ago: "God said it; I believe it; that settles it."

Blind Faith?

Someone may ask, "Isn't that blind faith? How can I accept something I can't prove?"

We have described biblical faith as a firm conviction that what God says is true, that what He promises, He can and will do. Even if those promises seem impossible according to human understanding, faith still trusts God. We may not be able to know God through our five senses, but through faith we can have complete confidence in His existence and involvement in our lives.

However, this statement of biblical faith is not the same as blind faith. Blind faith is believing something with little or no evidence. God has shown us over and over that His word is true and worthy of belief. There is evidence all around us of His existence and reliability. Once we recognize and accept this evidence, we will believe everything He says, because we know He is trustworthy. Therefore following God without further question is not blind faith; it is acting on what we know to be true, even though we may not be able to prove it by our five human senses.

Richard Batey explains it in this way:

> Faith for Paul is not without its critical faculty; to trust in God does not require a sacrifice of the intellect and a credulous attitude devoid of reflection. The doubt which arises when the promise of God is considered from a human point of view is not destroyed by faith but taken up within faith. Faith views the promise of God as the divine possibility which considered from man's own ability is impossible. Doubt should not give rise to feelings of guilt and become consciously suppressed, for doubt is that part of faith which makes absolute reliance on God necessary. (*Living Word Commentary on Romans* [Abilene: ACU Press, 1969] p. 62.)

We need to know **why** we believe in Jesus, **why** we trust God, **why** we should be faithful to Him, but we do not need to know **why** God gave every command.

Abraham did not know **why** God told him to offer Isaac – he only knew God told him to do so, and that was enough for him. Was this blind faith? No, Abraham had known God and His blessings for a long time, and thus he had ample evidence that whatever God said should be obeyed.

Even in the face of persecution and imprisonment Paul expressed this same kind of faith in God. "I know whom I have *believed*, and am convinced that he is able to guard what I have entrusted to him for that day" (2 Timothy 1:12). Paul's faith was not blind; he knew God and trusted Him.

As our involvement with God becomes longer, we should know Him better and be able to trust Him more. Our faith in Him is not blind; it is based on knowledge and experience.

The Importance of Faith

In John 6 we read about a multitude of people who followed Jesus for some time because of the miracles He performed. He fed them, then He walked on the Sea of Galilee toward Capernaum without a boat, and they followed Him again. Jesus confronted them by saying that the only reason they were following Him was because He had fed them and they were full. He told them, "Do not work for food that spoils, but for food that endures to eternal life" (v. 27).

Naturally they wanted to know what kind of work they had to do to get this food. Jesus told them, and us, that one of the most important things that anyone can do is to trust Jesus. "Then they asked him, 'What must we do to do the works God requires?' Jesus answered, 'The work of God is this: to *believe* in the one he has sent'" (vv. 28-29). God sent Jesus as His messenger to us. If we trust that messenger, we will also believe the message and the one who sent it. It is essential to our being Christians that we have faith in, or trust, Jesus as the messenger from God the Almighty.

The people following Jesus wanted to set Him up as a political king right then (v. 15); they did not understand what He was teaching. Many of them were legalists – they thought

that if they followed all the traditions exactly, God would accept them. They thought there were certain "forms" or "rites"
that had to be performed in a certain way, whether the heart
was in it or not. Rather than going into a long discussion of
God's love and man's response and freedom of choice, Jesus
answered them on their own level by telling them the core of
what God wants (not forces) them to do: to trust Him.

Some thought that the subsequent teaching concerning the
bread of life was too difficult, so they stopped following Him.
When Jesus asked the Twelve if they also wanted to leave him,
Peter answered for all of them: "Lord, to whom shall we go?
You have the words of eternal life. We *believe* and know that
you are the Holy One of God" (vv. 68-69).

The Greek word *pisteuo* indicates a stronger degree of cer-
tainty than our English word "believe." By "believe" Peter
did not mean, "Well, yes, we think you might be who you say
you are." No, he said, "We believe and know!" He said basically the same thing twice for emphasis. It was more than intellectual assent. The Twelve trusted Jesus to the extent that
they acted on their faith in Him by staying with Him even
though many other disciples were leaving him (v. 66).

Through Jesus, God has revealed Himself and His righteousness. We accept this by faith from beginning to end, and
we live our lives in this faith. We cannot be righteous without the faith that comes from knowing God through what He
has revealed about himself in Jesus and in His holy Word.
Without this kind of faith, we cannot hope to please Him.
"And without *faith* it is impossible to please God, because
anyone who comes to him must *believe* that he exists and that
he rewards those who earnestly seek him" (Hebrews 11:6).

Jesus emphasized the importance of faith, and this emphasis is continued in other passages, such as Galatians 5:6.
"For in Christ Jesus neither circumcision nor uncircumcision
has any value. The only thing that counts is *faith* expressing
itself through love."

Faith and Love

It is not enough merely to claim to have faith; that faith must
express itself; it must do something. As James says in 2:17-18,

"faith by itself, if it is not accompanied by action, is dead. ... Show me your *faith* without deeds, and I will show you my *faith* by what I do."

True faith cannot be hidden. Have you ever seen a small child so delighted about something that the laughter and giggles could not be stopped? Faith is like that. When we trust God, feelings of joy and relief and gratitude well up within us and must have expression as surely as a baby's giggle. In fact, it is easier to restrain a child's laughter than to conceal faith. Both well up from inside to demand expression. Faith will be obvious to others, not so much by what we say as by what we do – not with high-sounding words and protestations of abundant faith, but by the daily activities of life. What is important is our faith being expressed through love. This kind of love is action more than emotion. It is what we do rather than how we feel. Our faith is obvious in the loving way we treat others.

The connection between faith and love is further expressed in 1 Corinthians 16:13-14. "Be on your guard; stand firm in the *faith;* be men of courage; be strong. Do everything in love."

Standing firm means something more than merely giving intellectual assent to the facts of the gospel as revealed in the Bible. It is not passive; it requires some kind of action. It gets down to the essentials of our lives, how we act, the kind of people we are. Standing firm does not mean harshly condemning those who disagree with us; rather it means lovingly showing others the faith that guides our lives.

Thus we see that there are at least three meanings of faith, and all three must be present in our lives. One refers to the body of information revealed to us by God in the Bible. It is to these truths about God that we give intellectual assent, which is the second meaning. We must read and study our Bibles to know what we believe. "[F]aith comes from hearing the message, and the message is heard through the word of Christ" (Romans 10:17). The third meaning tells us it is not enough merely to accept these things as fact; we must integrate them into everything we do. As we trust in the truth of the message of Christ, we make this faith so much a part of our lives that it becomes what we are; we are full of faith. We act on our faith. We live our lives by faith and in faith. We trust God totally.

Three Aspects of Faithful

The Greek word *pistis* is also translated "faithful." In addition to the three meanings of faith we have discussed, there are at least three meanings of "faithful."

1. Consistently doing what is right. For example, when we carry out our assigned duties, then we are said to be performing our jobs faithfully. This meaning is illustrated in the parable of the talents in Matthew 25. The master entrusted three of his servants with varying amounts of money. Two of the servants invested the funds and gained more money for the master. Because they had done the right things, both were told by the master, "Well done, good and *faithful* servant!" (vv. 21, 23). The third servant was condemned because he did not do what was expected of him.

If we are faithful in doing what we should, we will keep on keeping on, even when it may not be what we really want to do. When no one is watching us, we will still continue just because we know it is the right thing to do. This aspect of faithfulness is PERSEVERANCE.

2. Consistently avoiding what is wrong. For example, if one does not engage in an extramarital affair, then that person is said to be faithful to his or her spouse. If we avoid doing things that we believe to be wrong, then we are being faithful to our principles. This is not merely following our habits or being in a rut. It is acknowledging by our lives the difference between right and wrong. This quality is an aspect of remaining true to our profession of faith. This meaning can be illustrated by the admonition to the church in Smyrna in Revelation 2:10: "*Be faithful*, even to the point of death, and I will give you the crown of life." God urged them to remain true to Him even in the face of severe persecution instigated by the devil. This aspect of faithfulness is LOYALTY or FIDELITY.

3. Faith-full or being full of faith. This meaning is the fundamental one. If we are full of faith, not only full of the facts of the gospel but also full of trust in God, then we will have the motivation to do what is right and avoid what is wrong. Faith will direct our lives. Because we know God and trust Him, we continue to do what we know is right even if we do not understand everything, and we consistently refrain from doing things that are not in accord with the principles of God. We must be full of the faith, the teachings of the Bible, in order to be full of trust, or faith, in God. We must be consistent in acting on our faith. It takes all of this to be FAITH-FULL.

Because the same Greek word is translated as "faith," "belief" and "faithful," we must look at the context in each instance to see how the word is used and to understand which meaning is indicated.

Stephen and Barnabas

Two men in the New Testament said to be full of faith are Stephen (Acts 6:5) and Barnabas (11:24). As we look at their lives we see their faith-full-ness demonstrated in several ways.

Stephen knew the Scriptures well. Acts 7 records the great defense he offered to the Sanhedrin in which he traces the history of the Israelites, showing how God had continued to keep His promises and demonstrate His faithfulness to them. Stephen was not ashamed to tell others about his faith. He continued to have faith even under persecution. He did the right thing, even when it was not easy. He trusted God and relied on Him to give him the strength needed to go on. Even at his martyrdom, Stephen had the spirit of unlimited forgiveness that Jesus taught.

Stephen's death was associated with persecution that scattered Christians away from Jerusalem. Some of them went to Antioch, preached Jesus there, and converted many people. When the leaders in Jerusalem heard about it, they sent Barnabas to the new Christians in Antioch.

> When he arrived and saw the evidence of the grace of God, he was glad and encouraged them all to remain true to the Lord with all their hearts. He was a good man, full of the Holy Spirit and *faith*, and a great number of people were brought to the Lord. (Acts 11:23-24)

Barnabas, like Stephen, knew the Scriptures well (vv. 22-26). He sold his field and gave the money to the apostles (4:36-37). He defended Saul in Jerusalem when the apostles there did not believe he had been converted (9:26-30). Because of the faithfulness of Barnabas, the other disciples entrusted him with the money they sent to Judea to help with the famine there (11:27-30). He was selected by the Holy Spirit to go with Saul on his first missionary journey (13:2). After Mark turned back, Barnabas gave him a second chance and took him on another journey (15:36-40).

Both Stephen and Barnabas showed by the way they lived that they were faith-full.

Live Faithfully

Hebrews 10 and 11 emphasize both the confidence we can have in our faith and the importance of our perseverance. A contrast is drawn between the old Law of Moses and the new gospel of Christ. In the early part of chapter 10, Christ's once-for-all sacrifice is shown to be far better than the endless animal sacrifices under the old Law. Because of this fact, the writer encourages his readers to be faithful:

> Therefore, brothers, since we have confidence to enter the Most Holy Place by the blood of Jesus, by a new and living way opened for us through the curtain, that is, his body, and since we have a great priest over the house of God, let us draw near to God with a sincere heart in full assurance of *faith*, having our hearts sprinkled to cleanse us from a guilty conscience and having our bodies washed with pure water. Let us hold unswervingly to the hope we profess, for he who promised is *faithful*. And let us consider how we may spur one another on toward love and good deeds. (10:19-24)

Notice the use of words such as "confidence," "full assurance," and "unswerving." The sacrifice of Jesus enables us to know that the promises of God are trustworthy. Our faith assures us that our hope is not in vain. Because of the confidence we have through this faith, we should encourage each other to show love and do good things. We should faithfully continue in the full assurance that is ours because of faith, and we should hold unswervingly to the hope that is ours because of the death of Christ. In other words, we should keep on doing what is right because we see that God has demonstrated the faithfulness of His promises.

Verses 26-31 also urge consistency in doing what is right. If we deliberately do wrong, what hope is there for us? Punishment will surely follow willful disobedience of God.

In verses 32-34 the writer reminds the readers of the way they felt when they first became Christians. They had a deep joy even in the face of persecution. They stood their ground; that is, they kept on doing the right things and believing the message they had received even though they were persecuted for that faith. They persevered.

The idea of faithfully keeping on is brought out even more clearly in verses 35-39:

> So do not throw away your confidence; it will be richly rewarded. You need to persevere so that when you have done the will of God, you will receive what he has promised. For in just a very little while,
> "He who is coming will come and will not delay.
> But my righteous one will live by *faith*.
> And if he shrinks back,
> I will not be pleased with him."
> But we are not of those who shrink back and are destroyed, but of those who *believe* and are saved.

The statement about the righteous living by faith is a quotation from Habakkuk 2:4, which is also quoted in Romans 1:17 and Galatians 3:11. What does it mean to live by faith? R. L. Johnson, commenting on Galatians 3:11, explains the quotation this way:

> A translation closer to the Hebrew of Habakkuk would be, "the just shall live by his steadfastness." The prophet was mainly thinking in terms of right living in this present world. ... The justified man lives by faith, and his faith gives him life. Faith moves on through God's righteousness to bless-

ing. (*Living Word Commentary on Galatians* [Abilene: ACU Press, 1969], p. 85)

When we live by faith, our faith influences all of our daily decisions. Everything we do is related to our faith and influenced by it. We cannot have separate compartments of our lives for faith and for other things. Faith must be in all those compartments. We want to do the right things because of God's faithfulness to us and our love for God. We want to receive the promises God has given us concerning salvation.

Faithfulness of God's Servants

Hebrews 11 contains a number of illustrations from the Old Testament of people who lived by faith. These were people who continued to do what they should because they were full of faith; they persevered. Perhaps by looking at a few of them we can gain a clearer understanding of what living faithfully means. This chapter is often described as the roll-call of faith; more accurately it describes the faithfulness of God's servants.

Hebrews 11:1-2 explains why the people named in the rest of the chapter should be held up as examples to us. "Now *faith* is being sure of what we hope for and certain of what we do not see. This is what the ancients were commended for." Biblical faith is confident assurance even of things that cannot be proved by sight. It is absolute trust in what God says and does. Those named in this chapter knew God so well that they could rely on Him, trust Him, know that what He said was right, even if they could not see the end result. They lived their lives doing what God wanted them to do, obeying Him because they wanted to please Him, and they were convinced that it was the right thing for them to do.

Verse 6 tells us that "without *faith* it is impossible to please God, because anyone who comes to him must *believe* that he exists and that he rewards those who earnestly seek him." This is not just a vague idea of "Well, yes, there probably is a Superior Intelligence that is up there somewhere, and maybe He sometimes dabbles in our lives, and maybe there is even something after death." No, this is a firm conviction about God's existence and His promises that makes us earnestly try to find out what He wants and then to do it.

Compare Hebrews 11:8-12 with what we have read about Abraham in Romans 4:

> By *faith* Abraham, when called to go to a place he would later receive as his inheritance, obeyed and went, even though he did not know where he was going. By *faith* he made his home in the promised land like a stranger in a foreign country; he lived in tents, as did Isaac and Jacob, who were heirs with him of the same promise. For he was looking forward to the city with foundations, whose architect and builder is God.

> By *faith* Abraham, even though he was past age – and Sarah herself was barren – was enabled to become a father because he considered him *faithful* who had made the promise. And so from this one man, and he as good as dead, came descendants as numerous as the stars in the sky and as countless as the sand on the seashore.

Abraham, believing that God was able to keep His promises, acted on his faith. He did not give up even though he never saw the end result. He left his homeland for a foreign country in obedience to God. He fathered the child of promise even though he knew it was humanly impossible. He persisted in his faithfulness to God because he knew that God was able to do anything He promised, even as far as making Abraham's offspring as numerous as the stars.

The faithfulness of Noah is also discussed in Hebrews 11:

> By *faith* Noah, when warned about things not yet seen, in holy fear built an ark to save his family. By his *faith* he condemned the world and became heir of the righteousness that comes by *faith*. (v. 7)

Noah believed God when He promised that a flood was coming, and Noah acted on that faith – he built the ark. The world may have laughed at him for building that big boat in the middle of dry ground, but Noah felt a holy reverence for God that encouraged him to continue working faithfully for years in obedience to God's Word.

Many other faithful individuals are named in this chapter. The Israelites as a whole are commended for their faith in crossing the Red Sea and marching around the walls of Jericho. Hebrews 11:13 sums up the idea of faithfulness as perseverance even though these people never received all the promises God made. "All these people were still living by *faith* when they died. They did not receive the things promised; they only saw them and welcomed them from a distance."

Although these faithful servants of God did not see the fulfillment of the promises, because of their faithfulness they were able to accomplish great things. Verses 32-40 refer to some of their stories:

> And what more shall I say? I do not have time to tell about Gideon, Barak, Samson, Jephthah, David, Samuel and the prophets, who through *faith* conquered kingdoms, administered justice, and gained what was promised; who shut the mouths of lions, quenched the fury of the flames, and escaped the edge of the sword; whose weakness was turned to strength; and who became powerful in battle and routed foreign armies. Women received back their dead, raised to life again. Others were tortured and refused to be released, so that they might gain a better resurrection. Some faced jeers and flogging, while still others were chained and put in prison. They were stoned; they were sawed in two; they were put to death by the sword. They went about in sheepskins and goatskins, destitute, persecuted and mistreated – the world was not worthy of them. They wandered in deserts and mountains, and in caves and holes in the ground.
>
> These were all commended for their *faith*, yet none of them received what had been promised. God had planned something better for us so that only together with us would they be made perfect.

They were commended because of their faith, their faithfulness, their perseverance. They kept on keeping on because they were faith-full. There must have been times when each of them was discouraged and unhappy. Yet even when prospects looked bleak,they had confidence that God would keep His promises in the end. They continued to hope even until their death.

This is not the kind of "hope" that we mean when we say such things as: "Oh, I sure hope I get a letter today." Our use of "hope" in this way really means "I wish." The biblical use of "hope" is much more than a mere wish – there is every expectation that the hope will be fulfilled. That is where faith enters the picture.

Faithfulness does not mean that we will never be dejected or that we will always be cheerful and upbeat. It does not mean we will always do what is right and never do what is wrong. Rather, it refers to the way we react to situations around us and what we do when we realize we have done wrong. Faithfulness means that we will not doubt that God is powerful enough to keep His promises in spite of how bad things are for us. It means that when we feel overwhelmed, we will look to God. Even when we sin, if we are full of faith, we will turn back to God when we realize we have done wrong.

What If We Do Something Wrong?

There are many examples in the Bible of persons who have sinned but are still said to be faithful. How can that be?

When God sent Samuel to anoint the next king over Israel, God wanted "a man after his own heart" (1 Samuel 13:14). Samuel wanted to anoint one of the handsome older sons of Jesse, but the Lord had not chosen any of them. He had chosen David, the youngest son. God explained His reasoning by saying, "The Lord does not look at the things man looks at. Man looks at the outward appearance, but the Lord looks at the heart" (16:7).

Even before David was anointed, God knew his heart and that he would be faithful. However, David was not perfect; he sinned. He committed adultery with Bathsheba, and he murdered Uriah, among other things. Yet even after these terrible sins, God later considered David to be a standard of faithfulness for the kings who followed him. For example, Amaziah did some things right but could have been better. "He did what was right in the eyes of the Lord, but not as his father David had done" (2 Kings 14:3). Ahaz was a king who was not faithful to God. "Unlike David his father, he did not do what was right in the eyes of the Lord his God" (16:2). Other kings were compared either favorably or unfavorably with David and his faithfulness. Considering the terrible sins David committed, how could God have been pleased with him?

The key is how David reacted when he recognized his sins. The Lord was displeased with what David had done to Bathsheba and Uriah. He sent the prophet Nathan to confront David. The story is told in 2 Samuel 12. Nathan did not immediately accuse David, but first told him a parable:

> There were two men in a certain town, one rich and the other poor. The rich man had a very large number of sheep and cattle, but the poor man had nothing except one little ewe lamb he had bought. He raised it, and it grew up with him and his children. It shared his food, drank from his cup and even slept in his arms. It was like a daughter to him.
>
> Now a traveler came to the rich man, but the rich man refrained from taking one of his own sheep or cattle to prepare a meal for the traveler who had come to him. Instead, he took the ewe lamb that belonged to the poor man and prepared it for the one who had come to him. (vv. 1-4)

Not recognizing himself in this story, David was incensed. He immediately proclaimed that this pitiless man deserved to die for the insensitive thing he had done, and he must pay four times the value of the lamb. Only after David was convinced of the injustice in this story did Nathan make his point. "You are the man!" (v. 7). As Nathan continued to apply this story to David, David saw himself and his sinfulness.

> Then David said to Nathan, "I have sinned against the Lord."
>
> Nathan replied, "The Lord has taken away your sin. You are not going to die. But because by doing this you have made the enemies of the Lord show utter contempt, the son born to you will die." (vv. 13-14)

David admitted his sin, and he was genuinely sorry for what he had done. When the child conceived in the adulterous relationship with Bathsheba became ill, David prayed, fasted and demonstrated his remorse (vv. 15-17), hoping to persuade God to change His mind (vv. 22-23). Yet when David knew the child was dead, he recognized that God had kept His word.

> Then David got up from the ground. After he had washed, put on lotions and changed his clothes, he went into the house of the Lord and worshiped. Then he went to his own house, and at his request they served him food, and he ate. (v. 20)

In David's sorrow for his sin, he turned to God. He had a contrite heart and he worshiped God. Although David had sinned, God forgave him, and he again became faithful to God as he continued his daily life. In the same way, when we sin, God is ready to forgive us when we turn back to Him. Our faithfulness is what causes us to continue to return to God no matter how many times we sin.

The apostle Peter is another example of faithfulness in spite of mistakes and blunders. Peter was one of Jesus' faithful disciples. Yet he, too, showed a lack of faith more than once. In Matthew 16 Peter found it difficult to accept some of Jesus' teachings:

> Jesus began to explain to his disciples that he must go to Jerusalem and suffer many things at the hands of the elders, chief priests and teachers of the law, and that he must be killed and on the third day be raised to life.
>
> Peter took him aside and began to rebuke him. "Never, Lord!" he said. "This shall never happen to you!"
>
> Jesus turned and said to Peter, "Out of my sight, Satan! You are a stumbling block to me; you do not have in mind the things of God, but the things of men." (vv. 21-23)

Although Peter had the audacity to rebuke Jesus himself, Jesus did not give up on him. Jesus took Peter, James and John to the Mount of Transfiguration with him (17:1-13). But even there Peter's faith lacked something when he suggested building three tabernacles, one each for Jesus, Moses and Elijah. God Himself had to correct Peter by saying, "This is my Son, whom I love; with him I am well pleased. Listen to him!" (v. 5). Peter needed to realize that only in Jesus should we put our faith, not in Moses, Elijah or anyone else. So Peter again listened to Jesus and tried to do what He wanted.

Nevertheless, after the Last Supper, Jesus told Peter that before the rooster crowed the next morning, he would three times deny that he knew Jesus. Peter protested that not only would he never deny Jesus but that he also was ready to die with Him (Matthew 26:31-35; Mark 14:27-31; Luke 22:31-34; John 13:37-38). Yet when Jesus was arrested, although Peter followed, it was at a distance.

When the cock crowed the next morning, Peter still had his mouth open from that third denial. "The Lord turned and looked straight at Peter. Then Peter remembered the word the Lord had spoken to him: 'Before the rooster crows today, you will disown me three times.' And he went outside and wept bitterly" (Luke 22:61-62).

Poor Peter. He had been so sure that he was ready to die for Jesus rather than deny Him. Yet in the few hours immediately following the statement of his intent, he could not admit that he even knew Jesus. When Peter heard the rooster and saw Jesus look him in the eye, how his heart must have ached! He knew he had not made it through even one night; and he wept bitterly (Luke 22:62). Peter had a contrite heart; it was broken for the Lord. He must have felt that he had failed so badly that there was no hope for him now – his life was useless!

Fortunately the story does not end there. When Peter reaffirmed his love, Jesus not only forgave him but also assigned him the important work of teaching others in the kingdom (John 21:15-19). Even something as bad as denying Jesus could be forgiven. Jesus knew Peter well enough to know that there was still much good that he could do.

Peter's life of service and faithfulness to Jesus was by no means over. Only a few weeks later he delivered a powerful sermon on the day of Pentecost. Throughout his life Peter continued to be faithful to Jesus, even though he was not always perfect. Paul found him to be in the wrong and corrected him (Galatians 2:11). Yet in the books of 1 and 2 Peter we see his emphasis on steadfastly holding to faith in God, even in the face of persecution. Just as Jesus knew Peter better than Peter knew himself, God knows us. He knows we will stumble and fail. But He also knows that we can again become faithful even after we have made serious mistakes. He is always ready to forgive us, to help us get back up, and to give us another chance. Jesus told Peter not to limit his forgiveness to others to only seven times (Matthew 18:21-22). If God expects unlimited forgiveness from us toward other humans, how much more will He forgive us! The key is that we want to do His will and that we keep trying.

However often these men of God sinned, they repented and turned again to follow God's way. Faithfulness does not mean that we will never make any mistakes. We do not always do what we know we should, we do not always do what we intend to do. We are like Paul when he said, "I do not understand what I do. For what I want to do I do not do, but what I hate I do" (Romans 7:15).

We are human and will do things wrong; we will sin. Nevertheless, our level of faithfulness determines how we handle ourselves after we realize and admit that we have sinned. If we are full of faith, we will continue to look to God for help, comfort and forgiveness. We will continue to love Him and to show that love by obeying Him. We will not rebel against Him. We will keep our hearts open to Him, and when we realize we have sinned, our hearts will be broken and we will turn to Him to heal us again.

Romans 14:1 is a very important passage for those of us who have been Christians for many years and should be more mature in the faith. "Accept him whose *faith* is weak, without passing judgment on disputable matters." Too often we expect a new Christian to have the same level of knowledge, faith, commitment and love that it has taken us a lifetime to acquire. We need to help and encourage, not condemn and argue. There will be times in all our lives when our faith will be weak, and we all need the help and encouragement of fellow Christians, the family of God.

Faith-full-ness

We have seen that a primary meaning of being "faithful" is to "hang in there," to "keep on keeping on" no matter what. Even if we do not feel like doing something, we should have the self-control to go ahead and do what is right anyway. However, this may be why some people misunderstand what it means to be a faithful Christian. They see someone doing the right thing, such as attending the assemblies of the church, and they assume that person is faithful. But we cannot identify faithfulness merely by externals. In fact, we really cannot determine the level of faithfulness of someone else; we can only guess at it by the fruit of their lives. It is up to God to judge each of us. We need to work on ourselves to determine and develop our own faith-full-ness as we try to live worthy lives.

Faithful Christians show their faith by the way they live. Faithfulness is not shown merely by regular attendance at church activities nor by a lack of overt wrongs. There is more to it than that. Faithful Christians attend church activities, such as the assembly, on a regular basis not merely because it is expected but because they want to experience the joy of assembling in God's presence with other believers to worship Him together. Being full of faith means not only being full of the facts of the gospel but also being full of trust in God, then continuing to obey Him no matter who or what tries to separate us from our faith in Him.

To be faith-full Christians, we must be full of faith in God and let that faith change our lives. We do the right things and avoid the wrong things, not out of duty or obligation but because of the faith that overflows our hearts. The more we read and study God's Word, the more we rely on Him in our lives, the more faith-full we will be.

If we stand firm in the faith, then we are faith-full. If we are full of faith, or trust, we know what God has done for us; and knowing what He has done in the past assures us that He will continue to act in our behalf in the future. If we know what He has done, we know Him. We can feel that personal relationship with Him that is so important in our lives. We do not worry that God will quit taking care of us. He is faithful; He will always continue to do what is right for us. We have no need to waver or doubt; instead, we are fully assured that God can and will do what He says.

Discussion Questions

1. From your experiences, how would you define faith? Faithful?
2. Relate your definitions and experiences to the definitions of faith given in Romans 4:21 and Hebrews 11:1.
3. Why is the resurrection of Jesus from the dead so central to your faith as a Christian?
4. What do you think are the essentials of faith for a Christian? What must you believe in order to be pleasing to God?
5. What can you do to strengthen your faith?
6. Is there any room in biblical faith for doubt? In what ways?
7. Discuss the relationship between faith and love. Use illustrations from your life.
8. In what ways did Stephen and Barnabas show their faithfulness? How can you follow their examples?
9. How can one who has sinned be considered faithful to God? How can a Christian become faithful again after having sinned?
10. What does the term "faithful Christian" (or "faith-full Christian") mean to you?

CHAPTER 7

Submission, What's in It for Me?

*"Submit to one another out of
reverence for Christ" (Ephesians 5:21).*

*M*any women today are saying, "Who, me? Submit to a man? No way! I'm as good as any man and as capable. Why should I submit to anybody? I'm a modern, enlightened woman, and I want my rights!"

Others are not so adamant, but are still saying, "Well, it seems to me that there is something to be said for equal rights for women. Aren't women important, too? Why do we have to submit to men? Can't we serve God effectively, too?"

The concept of submission as it is set forth in the Scriptures is sadly misunderstood today. Yet, it is a topic of major concern, both in the world and in the church.

Not long ago I overheard one man laughingly say to another, "My wife gets absolutely livid every time she hears anything about that submission nonsense." Because God's commands are never nonsense, she most likely does not understand what submission really is.

A Christian woman recently asked me, "Do you do everything your husband tells you?" How can one adequately answer that question in one or two words without leaving a wrong impression either way? It reminded me of another question that cannot be answered with a simple "Yes" or "No": "Are you proud of your humility?" Her question showed that she did not understand biblical submission any better than did the woman of the world.

The purpose of this chapter is to explore the meaning of submission – to look at what the Bible says about submission and to learn its significance in today's world. If we sharpen our perception of what God means when He says "submit," then we can more readily obey Him. We must first understand what God wants from us before we can do it ourselves or teach it to our sons and daughters.

Common Misconceptions

Several words and concepts are so similar in meaning to submission that they are often confused. Let us consider these before we try to define submission itself.

Neither Subordination nor Inferiority

Webster's Third New International Dictionary defines subordination as being "placed in a lower order, class or rank; holding a lower or inferior position." Subordination is a matter of position or status, while submission, as we shall see, involves something that one does as well as an attitude that one has.

Being in a subordinate position does not mean that one is inferior. The president of a large company who is occupied with executive decisions may send someone of lesser importance or value in the company, a subordinate, to run his errands. The president may actually have less ability, intelligence or wisdom than the employee, but it is his position in the company, not necessarily his person, that carries authority. The fact that the subordinate must follow the instructions of the president does not signify that he or she is of inferior quality.

In marriage God has placed the woman in a position that is subordinate to that of the man. However, the fact that God has ordained the husband to be the head of the wife (Ephesians 5:23) does not mean she is inferior to him. First Corinthians 11:3 also says that the head of Christ is God. "Now I want you to realize that the head of every man is Christ, and the head of the woman is man, and the head of Christ is God." This statement does not mean that women are inferior to men any more than it means that Christ is inferior to God. Other scriptures teach that Christ is equal to God. "Who, being in very nature God, did not consider equality with God something to be grasped" (Philippians 2:6). "And the Word [Christ] was God" (John 1:1). Thus we see that Ephesians 5:23 does not teach that women are inferior to men.

Galatians 3:27-28 states that both men and women are clothed with Christ in baptism and have the same salvation. "All of you who were baptized into Christ have been clothed with Christ. There is neither Jew nor Greek, slave nor free, male nor female, for you are all one in Christ Jesus." Although women may be placed in a subordinate position, there is no indication of second-class citizenship for women.

A person can be a subordinate without having a submissive attitude; also a person can be submissive without being in a subordinate position. Neither submissiveness nor subordination indicates inferiority.

Submission Is Not Subjugation

Webster says that subjugation is "to bring under the yoke of power or dominion; conquer by force and compel to submit as a subject to the government of another."

We can see the distinction between submission and subjugation in the Scriptures. In Hebrews 13:17 Christians are told to submit to their elders: "Obey your leaders and submit to their authority." Yet in 1 Peter 5:1-3 elders are told not to "lord it over," or subjugate, those who are commanded to submit to them.

Jesus said that the rulers of the Gentiles "lord it over" them; then He commanded His followers not to act that way, but to be servants (Matthew 20:25-28; Mark 10:42-45). Christians should submit to the elders, but the elders have no right to subjugate them.

Some people mistakenly think that because wives are told to submit to their husbands that the husbands have absolute rule and authority over their wives and thus are obligated to subjugate, or suppress, them. This idea is not what submission is, nor is it in agreement with other commands to husbands. Nowhere is a man given the command, or even the permission, to force any woman into submission.

Submission Is Not Subjection

Webster calls subjection "the exercise of lordship or control; ... the act of subduing, ... subjugation ... the quality or state of being subject, and esp. under the power, control, or government of another."

Subjection is close in meaning to submission, but there is a difference. Submission, as we shall see, is always voluntary, but subjection can be forced. Unfortunately, many translators use these two words interchangeably, thus obscuring the original meaning.

Submission Is Not Subservience

Webster defines subservience as "excessive willingness to submit to the control or demands of another; servile inferiority; useful in an inferior capacity; implies compliance and obedience, perhaps abject and marked by cringing, of one very conscious of a subordinate, dependent position."

Illustrating this misconception is the way Edith Bunker catered to Archie in the 1970s TV comedy *All in the Family*. Many people think that her actions constitute true submission. However, that is a very demeaning and unbiblical view. This misunderstanding of submission explains why some women become livid at the mere mention of the word.

Submission Is Not Capitulation or Surrender

Webster says that capitulation "centers attention on a definite act of surrendering or giving up to a stronger force or power." After struggling and fighting with her husband over some point, the wife may be tempted to say, "Okay, okay! Have it your way, I know you're going to anyway!" That is not submission nor is it God's way of solving problems in a family.

Submission and Obedience Are Not the Same

There is a difference. Suppose you have told your child several times to pick up the toys on the floor and put them into the toy box, but the toys are still scattered on the floor. You finally say in a calm, quiet, authoritative voice, "Pick up your toys **now**!" Your child, after realizing that you mean business this time, may obey you by picking up the toys. However, as you turn to leave the room, if the child's tongue is defiantly stuck out behind your back, that child is not showing submission.

There can be obedience without submission but not submission without obedience. Submission is obedience with proper respect, as in 1 Timothy 3:4. "He must manage his own family well and see that his children obey him with proper respect."

Perhaps the main difference between submission and obedience is that obedience is an action, while submission is an attitude. It is possible to perform an act of obedience without having a submissive attitude behind that action.

What Submission Really Means

After establishing some things that submission is not, we now turn to the positive side of submission. Webster defines "submit" as "to yield or bow to the will or authority of another; to grant precedence; defer." And "defer," Webster tells us, "strongly connotes yielding brought about by respect for another or for his position or authority." The word "bow" may be used to suggest "a party that has not been vanquished [yet] gives in or yields for politic or courteous reasons."

We can allow ourselves to come under the authority of another not because of weakness or inferiority, but because it is the best thing to do. Submissiveness is humble or compliant behavior, a voluntary yielding of power or authority to the control of another because of respect, courtesy or even just because it makes things run more smoothly.

It is to be emphasized that submission is voluntary, not forced upon one by the other. Remember, however, that although it is voluntary, it is commanded by God. In previous chapters we have emphasized that God does not force obedience, self-control or anything else on us. We ourselves must choose what we will do. The same thing is true of submission that is true of all the commands of God. We are free to choose, but we will receive the consequences, whether good or bad, of our choices.

Webster's definitions provide a better understanding of the English word "submit," but we also need to understand the meaning of the Greek word. A brief but important grammar lesson should help us. In English we use verbs in both active and passive voices. In the active voice the subject does something: "I washed the car." In the passive voice something is done to the subject: "The car was washed." In addition to active and passive, Greek has another voice, the middle. The middle voice represents the subject as acting either upon itself or for its own benefit: "I washed myself." This is similar to, but not identical with, the English reflexive verb.

The basic difference between the meaning of the middle voice and the meaning of the passive voice is that in the passive someone or something else does something to the subject, but in the middle voice the subject does something to or for itself, for its own benefit. The passages in the New Testament that refer to a wife's submission to her husband are all in the middle voice (Colossians 3:18; Titus 2:5; 1 Peter 3:1, 5).

The fundamental meaning of the Greek word *hypotasso*, usually translated "submit," is to "place or arrange under," thus in the middle voice it means to "place one's self under" someone else. This shows that submission is something the wife does for herself, for her own benefit. It is not the husband's place to demand or force her into subjugation. No one can submit another; one can only submit one's self.

Reciprocal, or mutual, submission is demanded of Christians in Ephesians 5:21. "Submit to one another out of reverence for Christ." As each submits to the other, each lifts up the other by willingly placing himself or herself under the other, and both are elevated as they build up each other according to God's plan.

In addition to the middle voice usage of the word for "submit," the Greek New Testament also uses this verb in both active and passive voices, but only in reference to God or Christ as the One who does the submitting of someone or something else. Only the Lord has the power to force submission.

"God placed all things under [Jesus'] feet and appointed him to be head over everything for the church" (Ephesians 1:22). "It is not to angels that he has subjected the world to come … 'and put everything under his feet.' In putting everything under him, God left nothing that is not subject to him. Yet at present we do not see everything subject to him." (Hebrews 2:5-9).

Philippians 3:20-21 refers to "the Lord Jesus Christ" and the "power that enables him to bring everything under his control." As we try to live worthy lives, it is the middle voice usage that concerns us most. We can control only our own voluntary actions; thus we need to explore those verses that tell us what we should do.

Submission should never be considered shameful. It is a character trait of Christ, and as such should be an important characteristic of His followers. Nor should a submissive attitude be deemed exclusively feminine. In 1 Peter 5:5-6 men are told to submit:

> Young men, in the same way be submissive to those who are older. Clothe yourselves with humility toward one another, because,
> "God opposes the proud
>   but gives grace to the humble."
> Humble yourselves, therefore, under God's mighty hand, that he may lift you up in due time.

What the Bible Says About Submission

In most discussions of submission, the only scriptures that are quoted are those dealing with woman's submission to man. However, this is only a small part of the total biblical concept of submission. The Greek verb for "submit," *hypotasso,* is used 38 times in the New Testament and only six of those times refer to a woman being in submission to a man. In addition, the noun form, *hypotage,* is used four times, only one of which refers specifically to women. As we look at the verses that use a form of this Greek word, notice the wide range of commands to submit.

The words translating *hypotasso* and *hypotage* are in italics in the following Scripture quotations.

The Whole Universe Is in Submission to God's Word

"For he [God] spoke, and it came to be" (Psalm 33:9). The stars and planets continue to be in submission to the power of God.

> My own hand laid the foundations of
> the earth,
> and my right hand spread out the
> heavens;
> when I summon them,
> they all stand up together. (Isaiah 48:13)

Nature remains under God's control. "It is the Lord who makes the storm clouds" (Zechariah 10:1). Many other scriptures also show that the universe is under God's control.

"For the creation was *subjected* to frustration, not by its own choice, but by the will of the one who *subjected* it" (Romans 8:20). This verse uses both passive and active forms of "submit," but remember that God is the only One who has the power to force someone or something into submission.

First Corinthians 15:27-28 also uses active and passive forms and makes it clear that all things are in submission to God:

> For he "has *put* everything *under* his feet." Now when it says that "everything" has been *put under* him, it is clear that this does not include God himself, who *put* everything *under* Christ. When he has done this, then the Son himself will be made *subject* to him who *put* everything *under* him.

Angels, Authorities and Powers Are in Submission to Christ

First Peter 3:21-22 tells of "the resurrection of Jesus Christ, who has gone into heaven and is at God's right hand – with angels, authorities and powers in *submission* to him." Because of Christ everything in heaven runs smoothly. In Revelation 21 and 22 we have a picture of the beauty and perfectness of heaven. It cannot be that way if those in heaven are not following the will of God.

Not only angels but also demons are submissive because of the name of Christ. Some of the disciples discovered this fact when Jesus sent them to tell about the coming kingdom. "The seventy-two returned with joy and said, 'Lord, even the demons *submit* to us in your name.' He replied, '... do not rejoice that the spirits *submit* to you, but rejoice that your names are written in heaven' " (Luke 10:17-20).

Every Person Must Submit to God

In James 4:7 we find a command to everyone. *"Submit* yourselves, then, to God. Resist the devil, and he will flee from you."* Notice the contrast between submission and resistance. The opposite of submission is rebellion. Deuteronomy tells of the rebellion of the Israelites against God that led to 40 years of wandering in the wilderness (1:26-44, and others). Rebellion caused problems for the Lord's people then, and rebellion will cause problems for the Lord's people now.

Romans 8:7 tells us that "the sinful mind is hostile to God. It does not *submit* to God's law." The sinful mind is the mind that does not resist the devil, but cooperates with him. Even if one is hostile to God in this life, he will still eventually submit to God. Romans 14:11 tells us that "every knee will bow before" God. We will acknowledge the power and glory of God either now or later. Our choice should be to do it now, when we can benefit from His blessings rather than later to receive His punishment. Hebrews 12:9 reminds us that "we have all had human fathers who disciplined us and we respected them for it. How much more should we *submit* to the Father of our spirits and live!"

We cannot submit to God unless we know what His will for us is. We tend to think that whatever we want is also what God wants. However, we must be very careful as we try to determine what God wants us to do. Romans 10:1-4 discusses some Israelites whose zeal for God was not based on knowledge. "Since they did not know the righteousness that comes from God and sought to establish their own, they did not *submit* to God's righteousness" (v. 3).

We study the Bible because it is there that we learn about God and His will. We should pray for His guidance as we try to make decisions according to His principles. We must be careful not to pay attention to persons who claim to know the Lord's will for us when what they say is not in agreement with what is in the Bible.

It is not enough merely to know God's will, we must also willingly obey it. God's love for us is so great that He demands only what is in our best interests. Therefore we should always have the attitude that when we learn what the Lord's will for us is, we will do it.

Even Christ Submitted to God

While praying shortly before His death, Jesus showed His submission to God. "My Father, if it is possible, may this cup be taken from me. Yet not as I will, but as you will" (Matthew 26:39). Although Hebrews 5:7-8 does not use the Greek word for submit, it still shows Christ's submissive attitude toward God's will for Him. "During the days of Jesus' life on earth, he offered up prayers ... and he was heard because of his reverent submission. Although he was a son, he learned obedience from what he suffered."

If Christ Himself was willing to submit to God's plans for Him, we certainly should also be willing to place ourselves under the authority of God.

Christians Must Submit to Political Powers

Several scriptures emphasize the importance of being good and obedient citizens. Paul tells Titus to "Remind the people to be *subject* to rulers and authorities" (Titus 3:1).

> Everyone must *submit* himself to the governing authorities, for there is no authority except that which God has established. The authorities that exist have been established by God. Consequently, he who rebels against the authority is rebelling against what God has instituted, and those who do so will bring judgment on themselves. For rulers hold no terror for those who do right, but for those who do wrong. Do you want to be free from fear of the one in authority? Then do what is right and he will commend you. For he is God's servant to do you good. But if you do wrong, be afraid, for he does not bear the sword for nothing. He is God's servant, an agent of wrath to bring punishment on the wrongdoer. Therefore, it is necessary to *submit* to the authorities, not only because of possible punishment but also because of conscience. (Romans 13:1-5)

> *Submit* yourselves for the Lord's sake to every authority instituted among men: whether to the king, as the supreme authority, or to governors, who are sent by him to punish those who do wrong and to

commend those who do right. For it is God's will that by doing good you should silence the ignorant talk of foolish men. Live as free men, but do not use your freedom as a cover-up for evil; live as servants of God. Show proper respect to everyone: Love the brotherhood of believers, fear God, honor the king. (1 Peter 2:13-17)

Christians should be the best citizens. We should do what is right, setting a good example for non-Christians who are watching us, and not do what is wrong, leaving ourselves open to punishment from the authorities. Christians act properly because of the Lord and our relationship with Him.

God established the concept of earthly rulers. When no one is in charge there is anarchy, but God wants peace and order (1 Corinthians 14:33). Submission to political powers is voluntary; we are told to submit, but the rulers are not told to subjugate. Unfortunately, not all rulers follow God's commands, but that does not negate our responsibilities. This submission to earthly powers must not violate other commands of God, as we see from Peter's statement in Acts 5:29: "We must obey God rather than men!"

God wants an orderly society. He has set up governments, which are not perfect (not even always good), yet we are to be law-abiding citizens. We must respect the authority of those who are over us.

The Church Must Submit to Christ

In reference to Christ, Ephesians 1:22-23 states: "And God *placed* all things *under* his feet and appointed him to be head over everything for the church, which is his body." Ephesians 5:24 tells us that "the church *submits* to Christ."

Common sense tells us that a body must act in accordance with instructions from its head. When there is a problem or a disease that makes it impossible for the body to respond properly to its head, then the whole person is dysfunctional. In the same way, if the church does not follow the teachings of Christ, then it ceases to function as the body of Christ.

Christians Must Submit to Church Leaders

You know that the household of Stephanas were the first converts in Achaia, and they have devoted themselves to the service of the saints. I urge you, brothers, to *submit* to such as these and to everyone who joins in the work, and labors at it. (1 Corinthians 16:15-16)

Although only this passage in 1 Corinthians uses the Greek word for "submit" in this connection, the concept is taught in several passages. Hebrews 13:17 uses another Greek word, *hypeiko* or "yield," that means basically the same as submit:

Obey your leaders and submit to their authority. They keep watch over you as men who must give an account. Obey them so that their work will be a joy, not a burden, for that would be of no advantage to you.

It is not enough merely to obey – there must be a willing attitude of yielding and submissiveness.

First Thessalonians 5:12-13 continues the teaching that Christians must submit to the leaders of the church:

Now we ask you, brothers, to respect those who work hard among you, who are over you in the Lord and who admonish you. Hold them in the highest regard in love because of their work.

The bottom line is that someone has to be in charge, someone has to be ultimately accountable. It is reported that President Harry Truman had a sign on his desk that read: "The buck stops here." He recognized and accepted his responsibility. If no one is in charge, there is confusion and chaos. This is true of churches, businesses, families and society in general.

Younger People Should Submit to the Older

After appealing to fellow elders not to be domineering over other Christians, 1 Peter 5:5-6 continues by addressing the attitude of all who are younger:

Young men, in the same way *be submissive* to those
who are older. Clothe yourselves with humility toward one another, because,
  God opposes the proud
  but gives grace to the humble.
Humble yourselves, therefore, under God's mighty
hand, that he may lift you up in due time.

Humility is closely related to submission in several New
Testament passages. Arrogance can never be a part of sub-
missiveness. The attitude of humble submission will allow
God to lift us up, to bless us, when the time is right.

Christians Must Submit to One Another

Ephesians 5:21 is plain. *"Submit* to one another out of reverence for Christ." This verse is part of a section in Ephesians
that emphasizes how we should live: "live a life worthy of
the calling we have in Christ" (4:1); "no longer live as the
Gentiles do" (4:17); "live a life of love" (5:2); "live as children
of light" (5:8); "be very careful, then, how you live – not as
unwise but as wise, ... understand what the Lord's will is; ...
be filled with the Spirit" (5:15-18).

This concern for how we live involves every moment of
our daily lives. It is not a now-and-then concern. It is not
how we act on certain days of the week or at certain times
of the day. It is the way we conduct ourselves all the time,
every day. We should live our lives in constant reverence for
Christ because of what He has done for us. All through this
section Paul relates our actions to the Lord. One major difference between Christians and other good moral people is
in the motivation: we do the right thing because of our desire to submit to God and please Him. This wise conduct expresses being filled with the Spirit.

Ephesians 5:18-21 shows that being submissive is not the
behavior of a person who acts according to ordinary human
nature but of the person filled with the Spirit of God. The
Greek grammatical construction of these verses is not obvious in most English translations, but it is revealing. "Be filled
with the Spirit" is followed by a series of participles, all dependent on the main verb "filled," which connects these acts:

"Speaking," "singing," "making music," "giving thanks," and "submitting." The King James Version closely follows the original in these verses:

> [B]e filled with the Spirit;
>
> Speaking to yourselves in psalms and hymns and spiritual songs, singing and making melody in your heart to the Lord;
>
> Giving thanks always for all things unto God and the Father in the name of our Lord Jesus Christ;
>
> *Submitting* yourselves one to another in the fear of God.

Thus we see that submitting to one another is an important part of being filled with the Spirit. It is also an indication that one is filled with the Spirit. We often hear these other things emphasized as important in the Christian's life, but submitting to one another is frequently ignored.

Under the heading of submitting to one another, Paul discusses three separate human relationships in which there must be mutual, or reciprocal, submission.

1. Wife/Husband. We finally arrive at the verses that are the most quoted on the topic of submission. "Wives, submit to your husbands as to the Lord" (Ephesians 5:22); "Wives, *submit* to your husbands, as is fitting in the Lord" (Colossians 3:18); "Train the younger women to ... *be subject* to their husbands" (Titus 2:4-5); "Wives, in the same way *be submissive* to your husbands" (1 Peter 3:1); and "the holy women of the past ... were *submissive* to their own husbands" (1 Peter 3:5). It is to be noted that in Ephesians 5:22 the Greek verb "submit" is not repeated from the preceding verse, but is understood. Thus verses 21 and 22 could be translated "Submit to one another. ... Wives, to your own husbands."

Yes, wives must submit to their husbands. However, if the husband carries out his part of the command (vv. 25-33), it will not be oppressive for the wife to submit. Remember that this is not subordination, subjugation, subservience, or any other misconception. It is submission.

The passages in Ephesians, Titus, and 1 Peter all include the Greek word for "your own" husband, thus emphasizing that this command is in the context of the marriage relationship only. Each wife submits to her own husband.

The Bible does not give a man the right to demand submission from his wife; rather it gives him the responsibility to treat her in such a way as to earn her respect, love, devotion and submission. The husband cannot force submission; rather he should act in such a way as to inspire it in his wife. She must submit, but he must never suppress.

Ephesians 5:25-33, dealing with the husband's responsibility to his wife, is sometimes overlooked when talking about marital relationships:

> Husbands, love your wives, just as Christ loved the church and gave himself up for her to make her holy, ... to present her to himself as a radiant church, ... holy and blameless. In this same way, husbands ought to love their wives as their own bodies. He who loves his wife loves himself. After all, no one ever hated his own body, but he feeds and cares for it, just as Christ does the church. ... However, each one of you also must love his wife as he loves himself.

A heavier burden is laid on the husband than on the wife. Although the wife must submit to her husband and respect him, the husband must love his wife in the same way that Christ loved the church. Christ submitted to death on the Cross for the good of His bride. That is a difficult example for men to follow, but a husband learns how to treat his wife by observing the behavior of Christ toward His bride, the church. Think of how much Christ loved the church and what a magnificent marriage it is when the husband loves his wife to that extent! It is easy to be submissive to that kind of love and devotion.

There is a beautiful story from ancient history about Tygranes, who was

> a prince or petty king in Armenia, whose land was conquered by Cyrus. He and his wife were con-

ducted into the presence of the conqueror, and the sentence of death was pronounced according to the barbarous custom of the time. Tygranes, however, pleaded with Cyrus that if necessary he might be exposed to double suffering and torture, in addition to his death, if only his wife might be spared and set free; and Cyrus was so pleased with the man's sincerity and earnestness that he pardoned them both. When outside the royal pavilion, Tygranes asked his wife what she thought of Cyrus, and she replied: "Indeed, I have no thought for him at all; I thought only of the man who said he was prepared to bear the torture and agony of death for me" (A. Gordon Nasby, ed., *Treasury of the Christian World* [New York: Harper & Brothers, 1953], p. 214.).

Can you imagine how willingly this woman would have complied with any request that Tygranes had for her? With that kind of love, submission could not have been a problem in their marriage. She knew he would never mistreat her in any way but would act only in her best interests.

In the ideal marriage the husband thoroughly loves his wife and puts her needs above his own, as Christ loves the church; and the wife willingly submits to her husband as the church submits to Christ. Yet we should not think of love as the husband's duty and submission as the wife's duty. Love and submission are so closely related that they must be considered two sides of the same coin. Each partner should lovingly and submissively consider the needs of the other before self.

Although Philippians 2:3-4 does not refer specifically to marriage, husbands and wives are included in the instructions. "Do nothing out of selfish ambition or vain conceit, but in humility consider others better than yourselves. Each of you should look not only to your own interests, but also to the interests of others."

The King James Version uses a little understood but rather enlightening phrase in Genesis 2:18. "And the Lord God said, It is not good that the man should be alone; I will make him a help meet for him." "Help meet" means a helper "fitting," "suitable for," or "answering to" the man. God intended for marriage to be the "meeting of the sexes" in the same sense that Eve was "meet" for Adam. He never intended it to be the "battle of the sexes." Each partner in the marriage should answer to the needs of the other and help the other in whatever way possible. If there is the mutual submission that God intended, each will lift the other to greater heights by placing himself or herself under the other.

If either the husband or the wife fails to live up to God's expectations, there will be problems in the marriage. God wants peace and order; therefore marriage should not be a battleground where one is trying to get the most out of the relationship for selfish reasons. Instead, both should be working for the good of the other and of the relationship as a whole. There is no room in marriage for selfish behavior.

A big part of mutual submission in marriage is compromise. Neither partner should insist that his or her way is best and that the other must change. Rather, each gives up something for the benefit of both, for the good of the marriage; they meet somewhere in the middle.

A college professor who enjoyed observing students commented that he could readily identify young couples who were really in love. As they walked across the campus, they would be in step without even realizing it. She would lengthen her stride, and he would shorten his to accommodate each other. They compromised. Without thinking about it, they were each submitting to the other in a small way. Their love was shown in the consideration each had for the other in making their walk together easier.

Headship of the man means that ultimately he is the one God holds responsible for the marriage and what happens in it. The husband must make the final decisions. His headship does not dictate the division of labor. God is not saying who writes the checks, who takes out the trash, who puts the children to bed, or who washes the dishes. However, for there to be peace and harmony, someone must be in charge, and God has decreed that in Christian families it is to be the husband.

God will hold the husband responsible even if he abdicates his role. Decisions should be made mutually, but if there is still disagreement after both have carefully and prayerfully considered all the angles, then the husband must make the final decision. The wife must have the attitude that because of her love and respect for her husband, and because she wants peace and harmony in their home as planned by God, she will support him in his decision. She should be able to have the confidence in him to know that he will do what is best for both of them.

Submissiveness should never be used to manipulate in order to get what one wants. Although a submissive attitude encourages the kind of love wives want from their husbands, it does not force it.

It is important to teach our sons to be the kind of men God wants husbands to be and to teach our daughters to be the kind of women God wants wives to be. A man should be very careful in choosing the woman he will love and cherish for the rest of his life. A woman should be just as careful in choosing the man to whom she is willing to submit for the rest of her life.

Wives should submit to their own husbands. Nowhere does the Bible teach that all women must submit to all men, although this misconception is prevalent. Two passages that are sometimes construed that way are 1 Corinthians 14:34: "Women should remain silent in the churches. They are not allowed to speak, but must be in *submission*, as the Law says;" and 1 Timothy 2:11-12: "A woman should learn in quietness and full *submission*. I do not permit a woman to teach or to have authority over a man; she must be silent."

However, there is evidence that both of these passages discuss the specific situation when the church was assembled as a church rather than referring to society as a whole. (Everett Ferguson, "TOPOS in 1 Timothy 2:8," *Restoration Quarterly*, Vol. 33/No.2 [1991], pp.65-73.) The submissiveness of women in these passages pertains to the assembly of the church, and mainly refers to submission to God's command that women be silent in the assembly. Here, the women's submission is to God, not to men.

It is to be noticed that 1 Corinthians 14:34 does not say, "as the Law of Moses says." Indeed there is no such law in the Mosaic code. However, Paul seems to be referring to Genesis 3:16 which says:

To the woman he said,
"I will greatly increase your pains in
    childbearing;
with pain you will give birth to children.
Your desire will be for your husband,
    and he will rule over you."

Thus it seems that if Paul is concerned with women's submission to men, it is within the husband/wife relationship rather than that all women should be in submission to all men. That the wife submits to her own husband is also shown by verse 35: "If they want to inquire about something, they should ask their own husbands at home."

That 1 Timothy 2 also pertains to the husband/wife relationship is indicated not only by the discussion of Adam and Eve but also by the reference in verse 15 to childbearing. Yet the prohibitions made by God in both these passages are not limited to wives, but apply to all women in the assembly.

Another passage that is sometimes quoted to show that all women should be in submission to all men is 1 Corinthians 11:3. "Now I want you to realize that the head of every man is Christ, and the head of the woman is man, and the head of Christ is God." However, there are several indications that this interpretation is not the meaning intended.

Although the context of this verse probably is not the assembly of the church, as 1 Corinthians 14:34 and 1 Timothy 2:8 seem to be, it still refers to some occasion at which women are permitted to pray and/or speak about spiritual things in the presence of both men and women. Thus certain conventions of propriety should be maintained concerning God's divine order.

The subsequent verses show that the emphasis is on the distinction between maleness and femaleness in appearance and therefore the roles that pertain to these functions. It is not a generalization of male superiority over females.

This passage may also be speaking of the headship of man in the marriage situation rather than in society as a whole. The Greek does not use the general word for "mankind" (*anthropos*) but uses the specific word for "male" or "husband" (*aner*) in contrast to the word for "woman" or "wife" (*gune*).

It should be further noticed that the singular is used: the "man" (or "husband") is the head of the "woman" (or "wife") and not that all "men" are the head of all "women." Therefore it seems that this passage is not talking about the dominance of men over women, but is instead talking about orderliness and propriety.

Even as God has set up political governments to which we must submit and which are not perfect in their actions, He has also determined an order in the family. Wives should submit to their husbands. God wants an orderly society both in the nation and in the home

2. Child/Parent. In Ephesians 6:1-4 Paul addresses the second relationship in the context of submitting to one another: "Children, obey your parents in the Lord, for this is right. ... Fathers, do not exasperate your children; instead, bring them up in the training and instruction of the Lord." Children and parents are also addressed in the parallel passage in Colossians 3:20-21. "Children, obey your parents in everything, for this pleases the Lord. Fathers, do not embitter your children."

Paul relates the child's obedience to the right attitude toward the Lord. The word "obey" (*hypakouo*) is used rather than "submit" in these passages, possibly because it is not natural for children to submit voluntarily to their parents. Children must be taught to obey even before they are mature enough to understand what it means to submit willingly. Submissiveness is not a childlike quality; it requires a measure of maturity.

Christ submitted to His earthly parents. Many English versions translate Luke 2:51 to say that Jesus "was *obedient* to" His parents. However, the Greek verb "submit" (*hypotasso*) is in the middle voice, thus indicating that He chose to submit to them willingly. This submissive attitude may not be natural to us, but it is one of the qualities of Christ that we should imitate in our own lives.

It is the responsibility of the parents, especially the father, to train the children in God's principles. In discussing what kind of man a leader in the church should be, 1 Timothy 3:4 uses the noun form of the word for submission. "He must manage his own family well and see that his children *obey* him with proper respect." This verse could also be translated that he should have his children "in submission."

It is not necessary for the father to handle all of the training and discipline personally. However, as head of the family it is his responsibility to ensure that the children are properly taught. The only way that children will learn to obey their parents is to be instructed. Although children must be under the control of their parents, the goal of discipline should be self-discipline, or self-control.

Parents must place the well-being of their children above their own interests. This is mutual submission in action. Parents must not selfishly demand only what they want without regard for the children's needs and wants.

Parents are not to be tyrannical or to exasperate their children. Sometimes parents say, "Do it because I said so!" or "As long as you are under MY roof you will obey MY rules!" This harshly expressed attitude will only make children eager to get away from such domination and will not encourage them to learn proper behavior.

The heavier load in the parent/child relationship is placed on the parent, as it was on the husband in the husband/wife relationship. The child is to obey because it is the right thing to do and because it pleases the Lord. However, the parent has the responsibility of lovingly training that child in such a way that he or she will know and follow God's will for a lifetime.

3. Slave/Master. The third relationship that involves mutual submission is that of slaves and masters.

> Slaves, obey your earthly masters with respect and fear, and with sincerity of heart, just as you would obey Christ. Obey them not only to win their favor when their eye is on you, but like slaves of Christ, doing the will of God from your heart. Serve wholeheartedly, as if you were serving the Lord, not men, because you know that the Lord will reward everyone for whatever good he does, whether he is slave or free. And masters, treat your slaves in the same way. Do not threaten them, since you know that he is who is both their Master and yours is in heaven, and there is no favoritism with him. (Ephesians 6:5-9)

There is a parallel passage in Colossians 3:22-4:1.

> Slaves obey your earthly masters in everything; and
> do it, not only when their eye is on you and to win
> their favor, but with sincerity of heart and rever-
> ence for the Lord. Whatever you do, work at it with
> all your heart, as working for the Lord, not for men,
> since you know that you will receive an inheritance
> from the Lord as a reward. It is the Lord Christ you
> are serving. ... Masters, provide your slaves with
> what is right and fair, because you know that you
> also have a Master in heaven.

As in the case of children, the Greek word in both Ephesians and Colossians is "obey" rather than "submit." Perhaps this is because slaves do not have the option of willingly placing themselves under the control of their masters. However, 1 Peter 2:18 does use "submit." "Slaves, *submit* yourselves to your masters with all respect, not only to those who are good and considerate, but also to those who are harsh." A slave may not be able to choose his master, but he can choose his attitude toward that master, whether the master is good or bad. We, too, are responsible for our attitudes.

We might be tempted to pass over this section by saying, "Well, we don't have slaves anymore, so this teaching does not apply." However, the Bible gives us broad principles for living, not detailed instructions. Because the slaves were the workers, it is logical to apply these principles to workers to-day. We need to look at the principles involved and see how to apply them to our lives. Just as Christians should be the best citizens, so Christians should be the best employees.

Titus 2:9-10 lists some very plain principles that all work-ers should follow:

> [T]each slaves to *be subject* to their masters in every-
> thing, to try to please them, not to talk back to them,
> and not to steal from them, but to show that they
> can be fully trusted, so that in every way they will
> make the teaching about God our Savior attractive.

We see from these passages that workers should be conscientious in carrying out their duties even if a supervisor is not watching them. They should work willingly and wholeheartedly, not merely for what they can get out of the situation and not merely doing as little as they can. They should work as if they are working for God Himself. It does not matter if the boss is good or bad, the workers should still do their best. Workers should be pleasant, courteous, trustworthy and honest. Notice that in every case the behavior of the worker is tied to the relationship to God and Christ. Submissiveness continues to be dependent on our spirituality.

Mutual submission between slaves and masters is also important. Slaves must obey masters, and masters must be considerate of slaves in the same way they want to be treated by the Master in heaven. "Respect and fear" (Ephesians 6:5) may refer to the feeling as well as the sign of that feeling. This kind of fear is not terror, but respect. It is the fear of God that was discussed in chapter 3, "That Awe-full Feeling." The principle that workers today should follow seems to be: Whatever you are supposed to do, do it right, as if you are doing it for God, because all that you do should be done for His glory. Do not do what is right just to win praise, but do what is right because that is what God wants you to do and you want to please Him.

The motivation for our actions should be what God wants. One of the most important lessons for any of us is that we must do everything God's way simply because it is right. We need to have the self-discipline or self-control to do what is right even if no one is watching. Think of all the problems in the world today that would be solved if everyone, slaves and masters, employees and bosses, students and teachers, citizens and law enforcers, families and churches would submit to God's plan of peace, harmony and unity.

God is a God of peace and order, not chaos (1 Corinthians 14:33). He has set forth these principles of mutual submission so that society in general, and the home in particular, will run smoothly and peacefully. We must abandon our selfish desires for the sake of the greater good. We will be richly blessed if we follow God's rules of submission in our daily lives.

What's in It for Me?

Although we should not decide to yield to God's will on the basis of the rewards we hope to receive, definite blessings are involved. Submission makes things operate in an orderly manner. Peace and order lead to a better quality of life, especially in our homes.

> Wine makes men boastfully self-important; it foments licentiousness, discord and strife, and is a troublemaker generally. Operating in reverse to all this, submission reduces the friction of life and promotes peace and comfort. Unnecessary trouble arises when somebody in home, business, or religious life, instead of being subject to others, in nonessential things, contentiously stands upon his own "rights." (R. C. Bell, *Studies in Ephesians* [Austin: Firm Foundation Publishing House, n.d.], p. 43.)

Submission promotes the well-being of those involved. If the home is in better shape, so are we.

> A Christian home is a place for husbands to learn to exercise authority graciously and wives to submit becomingly. It does not behoove two Christians, welded into one for life, as they pledge in their marriage vows, for the purpose of making a Christian home, the most heavenly achievement on earth, for the husband to exercise despotic authority or for the wife to yield slavish submission. When things go wrong in the home of worldlings, they have little recourse but alienation and divorce. If misunderstandings arise, as well they may, in the homes of Christians, they should be thankful for an opportunity to learn humility, patience, forgiveness, and love – all qualities they must learn somewhere, some way, sometime before they enter heaven (Ibid., p. 45).

Submission is an essential part of the Christian life; it is the way of life that we must follow if we are to be like Christ and inherit eternal life with him.

> Those who live according to the sinful nature have their minds set on what that nature desires; but those who live in accordance with the Spirit have their minds set on what the Spirit desires. The mind of sinful man is death, but the mind controlled by the Spirit is life and peace, because the sinful mind is hostile to God. It does not *submit* to God's law, nor can it do so. Those controlled by the sinful nature cannot please God.
>
> You, however, are controlled not by the sinful nature but by the Spirit, if the Spirit of God lives in you. And if anyone does not have the Spirit of Christ, he does not belong to Christ. But if Christ is in you, your body is dead because of sin, yet your spirit is alive because of righteousness. And if the Spirit of him who raised Jesus from the dead is living in you, he who raised Christ from the dead will also give life to your mortal bodies through his Spirit, who lives in you. (Romans 8:5-11)

We certainly do not want to be controlled by the sinful side of our natures, but by the Spirit of God. When we are willing to live by the Spirit, our lives are more meaningful and happier. If we do not belong to Christ because of our disobedient and rebellious choices, we do not receive the blessing of having Christ within us.

Hebrews 5:7-8 tells us:

> During the days of Jesus' life on earth, he offered up prayers and petitions with loud cries and tears to the one who could save him from death, and he was heard because of his reverent submission. Although he was a son, he learned obedience from what he suffered and, once made perfect, he became the source of eternal salvation for all who obey him and was designated by God to be high priest in the order of Melchizedek.

"Reverent submission" is translated in some versions as "godly fear." Godly fear is not terror but is more closely related to reverence and respect, which are necessary for submission. The prayers of Christ were heard from earth because of His reverent submission; therefore can we expect our prayers to be answered if we rebel against God's will?

Living in submission to God's will brings blessings to us. In 1 Peter 2:13-3:7 submission of several groups is considered. Then in verses 8-12 there are further instructions, based on the principle of mutual submission, with the promise of blessing:

> Finally, all of you, live in harmony with one another; be sympathetic, love as brothers, be compassionate and humble. Do not repay evil with evil or insult with insult, but with blessing, because to this you were called so that you may inherit a blessing. For,
> "Whoever would love life
>   and see good days
> must keep his tongue from evil
>   and his lips from deceitful speech.
> He must turn from evil and do good;
>   he must seek peace and pursue it.
> For the eyes of the Lord are on the righteous
>   and his ears are attentive to their prayer,
> but the face of the Lord is against
>   those who do evil."

Genesis 1 tells us that in the beginning there was chaos; everything was waste and void. God spoke, "Let there be," and whatever He said came into being. The elements obeyed Him and order prevailed. Even today, whenever God speaks to us and says, "Let there be ... in your life," if we accept His will for us, order will replace the chaos in our lives. Without God's rule in our lives, we are in chaos.

In the political world anarchy reigns when no one is in charge. God knows that in marriage someone needs to be in charge, so He commanded wives to be in submission to their husbands. When God speaks, we need to obey. If God had not chosen the one to be the head of the household, each couple would have to fight it out for dominance, and that would not be a peaceful situation. We may not understand why He chose the man, but that is what He did, and we should be willing to submit to His will in this matter as in all others. The happiest and most fulfilling marriages are those in which there is mutual submission, with the husband as the head of the family.

Our discussion has centered on the ideal of submission as set forth by God in the Bible. Of course it may be difficult to attain this, but unless we have that goal in front of us, we cannot strive for it. We must understand what God means by submission and what He wants from us before we can even try to attain it for ourselves or teach it to others. There may be many problems that stand in the way of our being truly submissive, but let us try to follow God's will in our lives. In that way we may be happy and blessed, and our prayers will be heard. Submission should be a way of life, not just for wives, but for all Christians in keeping with all the commands in the New Testament concerning this topic. We cannot be rebellious and still live worthy lives.

Discussion Questions

1. What is your definition of "submission"? Distinguish between what many people think it means and its biblical meaning.
2. Some people think that the main thrust of submission is that women must submit to men. Do you agree or disagree? Why? What do you think is its main thrust?
3. Why is the principle of submission important for all Christians? Give examples from your own life.
4. Why should Christians be good citizens? Why should you submit to the government even though it is not always what it should be?
5. How is being submissive related to being "filled with the Spirit" (Ephesians 5:18-21)? What other things are involved? How does this teaching affect your life?
6. What are the responsibilities of both husbands and wives in mutual submission? How does mutual submission work in your marriage, your parents' marriage or other marriages with which you are familiar?
7. What part does compromise play in a marriage? What sorts of things can be given up by each spouse without

compromising principles? Give examples from your experiences.

8. What does it mean to you for the husband to be the head of the wife?

9. From your observations, how is mutual submission reflected in the relationship between parents and children? How does it help parents train their children according to God's way?

10. How does the biblical teaching about behavior of slaves relate to the modern work force? How will this affect you at your job tomorrow, whether you are the employee or the employer?

11. In your life, what benefits have you seen in submitting to what is right rather than rebelling?

CHAPTER 8

*I*s It Really Worth It?

"Now to him who is able to do immeasurably more than all we ask
or imagine, according to his power that is at work within us, to
him be glory in the church and in Christ Jesus throughout all
generations, for ever and ever! Amen" (Ephesians 3:20-21).

*H*ave you ever been lost in a dense fog? Perhaps you were driving on a twisting mountain road or wandering by yourself in an unfamiliar city. Feelings of loneliness and insecurity may have been overwhelming: "Where is that road? Which way should I turn? How will I ever find my way?" If the road or city had been more familiar to you, then you would have felt more confident, even though unable to see your way clearly.

Sometimes our lives are foggy. We cannot see the right way to go. We know there is a road ahead of us, but we do not know which way it turns. However, that route is well known to us, our task is easier than if we are crossing unfamiliar territory.

If we know what the Bible says about the way God wants us to live, it will be easier to make the right choices in our lives. We need to study the Bible to see God's path for us – to know the difference between right and wrong. We should know ahead of time what God wants us to do, not just blindly meet each day with its temptations and problems. Then when we are in a fog we have a better awareness of the right way to go even when we cannot see everything clearly. We know to trust God, to rely on Him and His ability to lead us through the fog as we try to live worthy lives.

Sometimes, after we have struggled through a dense fog, sunshine and glorious scenery greet us on the other side. The beauty and peace that await us make all our efforts worthwhile.

The Lord has promised to be with us, in foggy times as well as in sunshine (Matthew 28:18-20). Again in James 4:8 there is the promise, "Come near to God and he will come near to you." What does it mean for God to be with us? Some of us think that if God is with us then everything will be all right; we will never be in a fog. We will never have problems or stress, we will have good health and financial security, our children will all be beautiful and well behaved, our marriages and other relationships will be perfect, and good luck will abound in our lives. But is that what God meant when He said He would be with us? Let us consider some biblical examples.

Does God's Presence Eliminate Problems?

In Illness or Death

Timothy was a servant of God, and there are many evidences that God was with him. Yet, we know that he had health problems. Paul advised him, "Stop drinking only water, and use a little wine because of your stomach and your frequent illnesses" (1 Timothy 5:23).

In the ancient world, wine for table use was normally mixed with water. The proportions varied at different periods of time and according to the purpose of the meal, but two or three parts water to one part wine was a common combination. When wine was added to the water, the alcohol in the wine killed the bacteria and thus purified the water. Taking a little wine with his water would help Timothy's stomach problems without the alcohol impairing his abilities. Timothy was in Ephesus, in what is now Turkey, and even today travelers are often advised not to drink the water.

We know that God was with Paul, yet he, too, had health problems. In 2 Corinthians 12:7-10 Paul talks about the thorn in his flesh. We do not know exactly what that was, but it was probably a chronic health problem that involved pain and suffering. The illness Paul mentioned in Galatians 4:14 may or may not refer to the same problem as his thorn in the flesh. Time after time we have all seen a good person become sick. We cannot say that God has deserted that person. Although God is with us as we try to live worthy lives, we will still have health problems and illnesses.

God's being with us does not mean that we will not die. Part of the cycle of life is death; all living things eventually die. God's plan from the time of Adam included the statement that dust would return to dust (Genesis 3:19).

Paul discusses the possibility of his own death in Philippians: "For to me, to live is Christ and to die is gain" (1:21). Paul knew that God would continue to be with him whether he lived or died.

When we face illness or death, in ourselves or someone we love, we cannot say, "Why me?" as if God has deserted us. Our encounters with illness and death are not dependent upon whether or not God is with us. Of course, there are instances in which the illness or death is caused by sin (drug or alcohol abuse, sexually transmitted diseases, etc.) or acts of irresponsibility or carelessness (stepping in front of a moving car, unhealthy eating habits, etc.), but these things are our own fault, not God's. Although we must accept responsibility for our actions, illness and death are not directly related to how good or bad we are.

God's presence does not eliminate either illness or death; rather He helps us with our attitudes toward these things. Ephesians 4:22-24 makes the contrast between life without Christ and life in Christ:

> You were taught, with regard to your former way of life, to put off your old self, which is being corrupted by its deceitful desires; to be made new in the attitude of your minds; and to put on the new self, created to be like God in true righteousness and holiness.

If we have godly attitudes, we will be better able to cope with the problems of life.

In Material Gain or Loss

God's being with us cannot be equated with financial success. Jesus never guaranteed riches to those who follow Him. He Himself had nothing, and He sent His disciples out with almost nothing. In fact, He said, "I tell you the truth, it is hard for a rich man to enter the kingdom of heaven. Again I tell you, it is easier for a camel to go through the eye of a needle than for a rich man to enter the kingdom of God" (Matthew 19:23-24).

It has been suggested that Jesus was referring not to a literal sewing needle but to a narrow gate in the city wall. This "Needle's Eye" earned its name because it was so narrow that it was difficult for a loaded camel to pass through. Yet Jesus says, "With man this is impossible, but with God all things are possible" (v. 26). This explanation implies that He meant literally the eye of a sewing needle. Although difficult, it was not impossible for a loaded camel to go through the gate. However, even though it was impossible for a man to make that same camel go through the eye of a sewing needle, God could do it.

Jesus' sense of humor was showing. The mental image of a big, fully loaded camel trying to fit through the eye of a small sewing needle is certainly amusing. To be filled with God's presence does not mean that we must go around with a long pious face. It is good for Christians to laugh. God has a sense of humor, and He wants us to enjoy life. He wants what is best for us in everything.

It is significant that Jesus did not say it is impossible for a rich man to enter heaven. Rather He said that "with God all things are possible." The difficulty arises when the rich trust in their riches more than in God. Although God has promised to be with us, He never promised us wealth or financial security.

In Stress or Ease

Paul certainly did not have an easy, stress-free life. His travels were much more difficult than ours today, and his service to God was filled with problems that we rarely have to face. He chronicled some of his hardships in 2 Corinthians 11:23-31.

Paul still could praise God after all these hardships – being in prison, flogged, exposed to death, beaten, stoned, shipwrecked, and in danger from many sources – because he knew

God was with him, helping him to endure these difficulties. God's blessings do not necessarily make our physical lives easier. Paul believed the promise Jesus made to His disciples in John 16:33. "I have told you these things, so that in me you may have peace. In this world you will have trouble. But take heart! I have overcome the world."

The Christians to whom the book of Hebrews was written were subjected to much stress and suffering even though God was with them. They could accept their persecution joyfully because they knew who was with them and what He had promised. They had faith in God's promises. They knew that the future held something better for them (Hebrews 10:32-34).

In 2 Corinthians 4:8-18 Paul wrote to the Christians at Corinth describing his situation and that of his co-laborers as they faced many difficulties while preaching the word of God:

> We are hard pressed on every side, but not crushed; perplexed, but not in despair; persecuted, but not abandoned; struck down, but not destroyed. We always carry around in our body the death of Jesus, so that the life of Jesus may also be revealed in our body. For we who are alive are always being given over to death for Jesus' sake, so that his life may be revealed in our mortal body. So then, death is at work in us, but life is at work in you.
>
> It is written: "I believed; therefore I have spoken." With that same spirit of faith we also believe and therefore speak, because we know that the one who raised the Lord Jesus from the dead will also raise us with Jesus and present us with you in his presence. All this is for your benefit, so that the grace that is reaching more and more people may cause thanksgiving to overflow to the glory of God.
>
> Therefore we do not lose heart. Though outwardly we are wasting away, yet inwardly we are being renewed day by day. For our light and momentary troubles are achieving for us an eternal glory that far outweighs them all. So we fix our eyes not on what is seen, but on what is unseen. For what is seen is temporary, but what is unseen is eternal.

Paul and his co-workers had many troubles, some of which are the same ones we endure today, yet Paul was sure that the eternal glory of being with God in heaven far outweighs any and all bad things experienced on this earth. The same principle is applicable for us today. We should not lose heart when things go against us because these things are temporary while God's presence is eternal. It is God's presence that renews us inwardly every day.

The Impact of His Presence

If God's presence does not mean an easier, trouble-free life, with good health and security, what then does it mean for God to be with us?

God's Presence Gives Us Strength

One blessing of God's presence is that it gives us the strength to deal with whatever problems we have. In the many different circumstances that Paul faced as he preached Christ, he learned a lesson that is as valuable for us as it was for him: "I can do everything through him who gives me strength" (Philippians 4:13).

A personal example of what it means for God to strengthen us will illustrate the point. Many college freshmen experience problems with roommates, homesickness, and many other things. I was no different. One evening I felt very much alone as I walked across the campus; my parents were far away, and I had no one to talk to, no one to care. The words of the song "My God and I" ran through my mind: "My God and I go in the field together, We walk and talk as good friends should and do. We clasp our hands, our voices ring with laughter, My God and I."

As I thought about these words, it suddenly dawned on me that I never have to be alone. God is always with me. At any time I can talk to Him, let Him help me with my problems, and feel His presence with me. He will help me make all my decisions. I can always draw upon His strength. When I realized this, I no longer felt lonely and deserted. I still had the same problems with my roommate, homesickness, and everything else, but now I had the strength to handle them.

That was one of the most valuable lessons I ever learned, in college or anywhere else.

First Corinthians 10:13 tells us that God will strengthen us even during temptations:

> No temptation has seized you except what is common to man. And God is faithful; he will not let you be tempted beyond what you can bear. But when you are tempted, he will also provide a way out so that you can stand up under it.

Some individuals may say, "But that verse is talking about temptations, and we are talking about the trials and stresses of life." However, many of our problems are brought upon us when we give in to temptations, and the principle is the same: God will provide a way out so that we can stand up under whatever problems we have. One of the main avenues out of temptation or problems is through prayer.

God promises to be with us, but He does not promise that life will always be smooth and easy. However, if we are faithful to the end, heaven will be smooth and easy – no problems, no cares, no troubles, no tears, no woes – only God in His glory and our eternal life with Him. On this earth we have to learn to deal with our problems; only in heaven will there be no problems. Although the greatest blessing of all will be eternal life in heaven with God, we also have blessings on this earth because of God's presence with us.

In John 10:7-10 Jesus compared Himself to the gate of the sheepfold. Through that gate the sheep find life; they come into the fold for safekeeping and go out to find pasture. They must have both protection and nourishment – protection from wild animals and robbers and the nourishment of food and water. It is through Jesus Christ that we find both protection and nourishment – protection from the devil and the worldly influences that tempt us and nourishment of the bread of life (6:35-59) and of the living water (4:10-14).

In John 10:10 Jesus says, "I have come that they may have life, and have it to the full." Other translations refer to having life "abundantly." Because of Him we can live our lives abundantly, to the fullest. It is only in Christ that we find the fullest meaning for our lives. It is only in Christ that we find spiritual fulfillment.

God's Presence Gives Us Peace

Another blessing of God's presence is that we have a deep inner peace that can be attained in no other way. Philippians 4:4-9 promises us this peace that we cannot understand:

> Rejoice in the Lord always. I will say it again: Rejoice! Let your gentleness be evident to all. The Lord is near. Do not be anxious about anything, but in everything, by prayer and petition, with thanksgiving, present your requests to God. And the peace of God, which transcends all understanding, will guard your hearts and your minds in Christ Jesus.
>
> Finally, brothers, whatever is true, whatever is noble, whatever is right, whatever is pure, whatever is lovely, whatever is admirable – if anything is excellent or praiseworthy – think about such things. Whatever you have learned or received or heard from me, or seen in me – put it into practice. And the God of peace will be with you.

We may not be able to understand or explain this peace, but we can experience it as we live our lives in the right relationship with God. As we continue to try to do what is right, we feel His peace.

This inner peace is also promised in Romans 5:1-5:

> Therefore, since we have been justified through faith, we have peace with God through our Lord Jesus Christ, through whom we have gained access by faith into this grace in which we now stand. And we rejoice in the hope of the glory of God. Not only so, but we also rejoice in our sufferings, because we know that suffering produces perseverance; perseverance, character; and character, hope. And hope does not disappoint us, because God has poured out his love into our hearts by the Holy Spirit, whom he has given us.

Although we may not be able to recognize it at the time, the difficulties that we conquer often make us stronger. We need to continue to trust God and persevere in doing right because He continues to love us and to be with us.

James 1:2-3 also shows us the importance of facing our problems with the right attitudes:

> Consider it pure joy, my brothers, whenever you face trials of many kinds, because you know that the testing of your faith develops perseverance. Perseverance must finish its work so that you may be mature and complete, not lacking anything.

God's Presence Gives Us Joy

Not only does God's presence give us peace, but it also gives us joy and hope. "May the God of hope fill you with all joy and peace as you trust in him, so that you may overflow with hope by the power of the Holy Spirit" (Romans 15:13).

There is joy in living a worthy life, but that does not mean we will always be laughing and jolly. Joy is not linked exclusively to frivolity, laughter or bubbly good times. We have already seen that God does not promise us smooth sailing on life's seas. There will be problems and hardships. However, knowing that God is with us will give us an inner peace that we cannot understand and a confidence that can be described as joy and happiness. We can contrast this peace with the emptiness and hopelessness felt by those with the same problems but without the comfort and support promised by God.

Biblical joy is based on the confidence we have in the message that Jesus Christ came to this earth to live among us in the flesh, to die on the cross to atone for all our sins, to be raised from the dead in triumph over the devil, and to ascend to heaven to prepare a place for our souls throughout all eternity. Joy is that inner sense of peace, well-being or happiness we have when we turn away from doing wrong and do what God says is right. It is also the feeling we have when we see others turning from lives of sin to lives of service to God.

Although biblical joy is difficult to define, many passages in the New Testament speak of it. The joy of being in God's kingdom is shown in Matthew 13:44-46. Nothing we have, or can ever have, is greater than or more important than this.

> The kingdom of heaven is like treasure hidden in a field. When a man found it, he hid it again, and then in his joy went and sold all he had and bought that field.
>
> Again, the kingdom of heaven is like a merchant looking for fine pearls. When he found one of great value, he went away and sold everything he had and bought it.

Both of these men made major changes in their lives in order to attain the treasure they found. We, too, will have to get rid of those things in our lives that prevent us from receiving the precious treasure of being under God's rule.

Christ found joy in loving and obeying His father. He wants us to know that same joy.

> As the Father has loved me, so have I loved you. Now remain in my love. If you obey my commands, you will remain in my love, just as I have obeyed my Father's commands and remain in his love. I have told you this so that my joy may be in you and that your joy may be complete. My command is this: Love each other as I have loved you. ... Everything that I learned from my Father I have made known to you. ... This is my command: Love each other. (John 15:9-17)

Jesus spoke these words shortly before His death. He was trying to prepare His disciples for all that was coming. He knew that He would face pain and anguish on the cross and that His disciples would also face problems in life, but He wanted them, and us, to have the joy of loving and being loved by God. Joy is found in our relationship with God. This relationship is maintained by our obedience to Him, just as our love for Him is shown in our obedience.

John 17:13 is part of a prayer to the Father that Jesus prayed shortly before His death. "I am coming to you now, but I say these things while I am still in the world, so that they may have the full measure of my joy within them." Jesus wants all of us to know the joy of living His way. It is only through His Word that we can learn how He wants us to live. We often think only of the agony Jesus suffered on the cross, but Hebrews 12:2-3 also shows the joy and triumph of the Cross:

> Let us fix our eyes on Jesus, the author and perfecter of our faith, who for the joy set before him endured the cross, scorning its shame, and sat down at the right hand of the throne of God. Consider him who endured such opposition from sinful men, so that you will not grow weary and lose heart.

It may be difficult for us to see how joy can be connected with the suffering and shame of the cross, but Jesus knew that it was only through His sacrifice that we could have salvation. His love for us is so great that He could find joy in knowing that His suffering was for our benefit. We, too, can find joy at the Cross as we realize the depth of what Christ has done for us.

Sometimes Christians must share in the sufferings of Christ. Although most of us do not face severe persecutions, there are still some who do. Anyone who is persecuted needs to have the attitudes expressed in 1 Peter 4:12-17:

> Dear friends, do not be surprised at the painful trial you are suffering, as though something strange were happening to you. But rejoice that you participate in the sufferings of Christ, so that you may be overjoyed when his glory is revealed. If you are insulted because of the name of Christ, you are blessed, for the Spirit of glory and of God rests on you. If you suffer, it should not be as a murderer or thief or any other kind of criminal, or even as a meddler. However, if you suffer as a Christian, do not be ashamed, but praise God that you bear that name. For it is time for judgment to begin with the family of God; and if it begins with us, what will the outcome be for those who do not obey the gospel of God?

If these persecutions are because we are Christians, then we
are blessed to have a part in revealing the glory of God. But if
we face difficulties caused by our lack of obedience to the
gospel, then we are not blessed, and we should be ashamed.

Acts 16:29-34 records the story of the Philippian jailer. He
and his family heard the word of God preached by Paul and
Silas. They believed it, they obeyed it, and they found the joy
that Jesus wanted them to have. The faith that the jailer and
his family now embraced through their obedience allowed
them to feel the joy of their new relationship with God.

Years later, while again in prison for preaching Christ, Paul
wrote a beautiful letter to the church in Philippi. How could
he write a letter so filled with joy and rejoicing when he had
suffered so many hardships? He obviously knew that the joy
he felt in serving God was not tied to external circumstances,
but was a result of his relationship with Christ Jesus. It was
because of the joy that he found in that relationship that he
could urge the Philippians to rejoice and be joyful in every
situation. He could also praise God in the midst of all the trials and difficulties that beset him.

God's Presence Helps Us to Live Worthily

A number of passages in the New Testament give a summary of some of the important aspects of living the Christian
life. One of them is Romans 12:9-19. Joy and rejoicing are included among these other items, all of which are important
as we try to live worthy lives:

> Love must be sincere. Hate what is evil; cling to
> what is good. Be devoted to one another in broth-
> erly love. Honor one another above yourselves.
> Never be lacking in zeal, but keep your spiritual
> fervor, serving the Lord. Be joyful in hope, patient
> in affliction, faithful in prayer. Share with God's
> people who are in need. Practice hospitality.
>
> Bless those who persecute you; bless and do not
> curse. Rejoice with those who rejoice; mourn with
> those who mourn. Live in harmony with one an-
> other. Do not be proud, but be willing to associate
> with people of low position. Do not be conceited.

Do not repay anyone evil for evil. Be careful to do what is right in the eyes of everybody. If it is possible, as far as it depends on you, live at peace with everyone. Do not take revenge, my friends, but leave room for God's wrath.

In earlier chapters we talked about the importance of learning and doing God's will. First Thessalonians 5:16-18 shows that God really does want us to be happy and wants what is best for us. "Be joyful always; pray continually; give thanks in all circumstances, for this is God's will for you in Christ Jesus."

Matthew 5:3-12 lists some of the blessings that are ours when we live according to God's way. Other translations for "blessed" are "happy" and "fortunate," especially in the sense of "privileged recipient of divine favor" (Bauer's Greek-English Lexicon).

Blessed are the poor in spirit,
    for theirs is the kingdom of heaven.
Blessed are those who mourn,
    for they will be comforted.
Blessed are the meek,
    for they will inherit the earth.
Blessed are those who hunger and thirst for
    righteousness,
    for they will be filled.
Blessed are the merciful,
    for they will be shown mercy.
Blessed are the pure in heart,
    for they will see God.
Blessed are the peacemakers,
    for they will be called sons of God.
Blessed are those who are persecuted because of
    righteousness,
    for theirs is the kingdom of heaven.
Blessed are you when people insult you,
    persecute you and falsely say all kinds of evil
    against you because of me. Rejoice and be glad,
    because great is your reward in heaven, for in
    the same way they persecuted the prophets
    who were before you.

These verses reinforce the idea that following God's way is the best and happiest way for us. Unhappy times will come, times of mourning and even of persecution, but God's blessings will comfort us, fill us, and cause us to rejoice.

God's Presence Gives Us the Hope of Salvation

In 1 Peter 1:3-9 we see the goal of our life on this earth – eternal life in heaven with God:

> Praise be to the God and Father of our Lord Jesus Christ! In his great mercy he has given us new birth into a living hope through the resurrection of Jesus Christ from the dead, and into an inheritance that can never perish, spoil or fade – kept in heaven for you, who through faith are shielded by God's power until the coming of the salvation that is ready to be revealed in the last time. In this you greatly rejoice, though now for a little while you may have had to suffer grief in all kinds of trials. These have come so that your faith – of greater worth than gold, which perishes even though refined by fire – may be proved genuine and may result in praise, glory and honor when Jesus Christ is revealed. Though you have not seen him, you love him; and even though you do not see him now, you believe in him and are filled with an inexpressible and glorious joy, for you are receiving the goal of your faith, the salvation of your souls.

Hope, faith and joy are interrelated on the journey to our inheritance. Although we may feel we are traveling through a fog, the hope of salvation is not a vague wish that things will turn out all right in the end. Rather it is a firm conviction, a confident faith, that God can give what He has promised to those whose faith is genuine and whose love is expressed even in suffering. Suffering for our faith strengthens our faith. The joy we feel is great, even when we are surrounded by grief, trials and fog. Salvation is the ultimate goal of our faith, but we also begin receiving the blessings of salvation even in this life.

God's presence gives the guidance and direction that leads us to salvation. Hope for eternal life with God gives purpose to our lives.

Is Living a Worthy Life Worth the Effort?

Living a worthy life is considered too hard by some people. However, most of the same stresses, problems and difficulties are encountered by both Christians and non-Christians. The main difference is that the Christian has God on his side, and thus the Christian's life becomes much easier and more filled with joy.

Psalm 19:7-11 makes it plain that God's way is the best way:

> The law of the Lord is perfect,
>   reviving the soul.
> The statutes of the Lord are trustworthy,
>   making wise the simple.
> The precepts of the Lord are right,
>   giving joy to the heart.
> The commands of the Lord are radiant,
>   giving light to the eyes.
> The fear of the Lord is pure,
>   enduring forever.
> The ordinances of the Lord are sure
>   and altogether righteous.
> They are more precious than gold,
>   than much pure gold;
> they are sweeter than honey,
>   than honey from the comb.
> By them is your servant warned;
>   in keeping them there is great reward.

It should be obvious that there is great reward in keeping laws that are perfect, trustworthy, right, radiant, pure, righteous, precious and sweet.

Paul tried to live a worthy life, but he was constantly beset by problems and persecutions, as recorded in 2 Corinthians 11:23-31. Did he think living the Christian life was worth all

these terrible things? Part of his answer to that question is in
2 Corinthians 12:9-10:

> I will boast all the more gladly about my weak-
> nesses, so that Christ's power may rest on me. That
> is why, for Christ's sake, I delight in weaknesses, in
> insults, in hardships, in persecutions, in difficulties.
> For when I am weak, then I am strong.

Another part of the answer is found in 1 Timothy 1:12-17:

> I thank Christ Jesus our Lord, who has given me
> strength, that he considered me faithful, appointing
> me to his service. Even though I was once a blas-
> phemer and a persecutor and a violent man, I was
> shown mercy because I acted in ignorance and un-
> belief. The grace of our Lord was poured out on me
> abundantly, along with the faith and love that are
> in Christ Jesus.
>
> Here is a trustworthy saying that deserves full ac-
> ceptance: Christ Jesus came into the world to save
> sinners – of whom I am the worst. But for that very
> reason I was shown mercy so that in me, the worst
> of sinners, Christ Jesus might display his unlimited
> patience as an example for those who would believe
> on him and receive eternal life. Now to the King eter-
> nal, immortal, invisible, the only God, be honor and
> glory for ever and ever. Amen.

Yes, Paul thought living a worthy life, a life in the presence
of God, was worth whatever hardships he had endured. Those
difficulties were nothing compared with the richness of the
blessings he received from God. In Philippians 3:7-11 he makes
this point very forcefully.

> But whatever was to my profit I now consider loss
> for the sake of Christ. What is more, I consider
> everything a loss compared to the surpassing great-
> ness of knowing Christ Jesus my Lord, for whose
> sake I have lost all things. I consider them rubbish,
> that I may gain Christ and be found in him, not hav-
> ing a righteousness of my own that comes from the

law, but that which is through faith in Christ – the righteousness that comes from God and is by faith. I want to know Christ and the power of his resurrection and the fellowship of sharing in his sufferings, becoming like him in his death, and so, somehow, to attain to the resurrection from the dead.

Paul realized that whatever honors, respect and physical comforts he enjoyed before his conversion to Christ were nothing compared with the unsearchable riches he had as a child of God. He would rather know Christ and serve Him than accomplish anything else in this world. He had learned that he could never do anything by himself to earn righteousness. He knew that only in Christ could he find that which is really important.

In Romans 6, Paul makes the point that when the Christians to whom he was writing were living in sin, the things they were doing brought them no benefits. Yet once they turned to God in obedience, they reaped Godly benefits (vv. 20-23). A life of holiness is far better than a life of slavery to sin.

Paul's plea was that others would also realize the blessings of God's presence in their lives. In 2 Timothy 1:7-12 he urged others to declare boldly the truths about our Lord:

For God did not give us a spirit of timidity, but a spirit of power, of love and of self-discipline.
So do not be ashamed to testify about our Lord, or ashamed of me his prisoner. But join with me in suffering for the gospel, by the power of God, who has saved us and called us to a holy life – not because of anything we have done but because of his own purpose and grace. This grace was given us in Christ Jesus before the beginning of time, but it has now been revealed through the appearing of our Savior, Christ Jesus, who has destroyed death and has brought life and immortality to light through the gospel. And of this gospel I was appointed a herald and an apostle and a teacher. That is why I am suffering as I am. Yet I am not ashamed, because I know whom I have believed,

and am convinced that he is able to guard what I have entrusted to him for that day.

Paul spent his life telling others about the marvelous blessings he had found in Christ Jesus. We should never be timid about telling others about God. Nevertheless, too often we spend our energies trying to get others to do what we think they should do. We tell them, "You must do this, this and this. You must not do that and that." However, the emphasis in the New Testament on evangelism involves telling others the Good News about Jesus Christ, not delivering to them a list of do's and don'ts. Christ must be the focal point of our message. We should tell how God has acted on our behalf all through history and how He has sent His Son to save us. We should not hesitate to tell others what God has done for us, in spite of any difficulties involved. Then they must act on that message from their hearts.

Because of Paul's faith in Jesus and in God, he was able to endure the many hardships he faced. He knew that his life with God, even with all its suffering, was much better than whatever kind of life he would have had without God.

Ephesians 1:3-10 expresses some of the blessing that we have and the praise that we should give to God:

> Praise be to the God and Father of our Lord Jesus Christ, who has blessed us in the heavenly realms with every spiritual blessing in Christ. For he chose us in him before the creation of the world to be holy and blameless in his sight. In love he predestined us to be adopted as his sons through Jesus Christ, in accordance with his pleasure and will – to the praise of his glorious grace, which he has freely given us in the One he loves. In him we have redemption through his blood, the forgiveness of sins, in accordance with the riches of God's grace that he lavished on us with all wisdom and understanding. And he made known to us the mystery of his will according to his good pleasure, which he purposed in Christ, to be put into effect when the times will have reached their fulfillment – to

bring all things in heaven and on earth together under one head, even Christ.

Yes, Paul's physical life was hard, but his spiritual life was full of rich blessings from God. These same blessings are not limited to biblical times and people. We face many of the same difficulties today, and God's blessings are still available for us. I am reminded of a dear friend who had been taught as religious truths things that were in conflict with the Bible. He began reading the Bible for himself and discovered that the things he had always believed, and indeed had taught to others, were not true. He accepted God's Word as truth and started trying to follow the teachings of the Bible rather than the teachings of men. His family rejected him. His friends rejected him. His former employer fired him. He had difficulty finding other work. His life seemed to cave in on him. Yet he continued to read and study the Bible and to trust in God. The more he learned about God, the firmer was his conviction that he was doing the right thing. Eventually he found other individuals who were also seeking to follow God's way rather than man's way. He thus found a new set of friends, a new family of believers, a new job and a great feeling of peace with God. For the rest of his life he joyfully and fully served the Lord, teaching others the Bible and the glory of God.

In many ways my friend reminded me of the apostle Paul. At first he fought against the truth, then he accepted it and spent his life ignoring the hardships that came to him while doing the will of the Lord. He knew that God was with him, and that gave him the strength to do what he knew was right. This friend was a very gracious and humble man, who led many sinners to God. If you had asked him if he thought living the Christian life was worth all the pain and suffering he had endured, he would not have hesitated to assure you that living a life worthy of God is the best, and indeed the only, way to go!

He probably would also have admitted that his early life was lived in a fog and that when he had struggled through the fog to the sunshine of the other side, he found true meaning for his life.

God Sets High Standards for Us

God wants us to be as much like Him as possible, and being like Him includes being pure and holy in all aspects of our lives. This purity must stem from the purity of our hearts and minds. We know we can never in this life be completely pure, but with God's help we can aim in that direction. When we stumble, God picks us up and sets us on the right path again if we will let Him. We must fill our minds with pure thoughts, and then let those thoughts control our actions. We must be holy, because God is holy.

Following God's way is not something we do to get something we want. God does not want us to obey Him in order to get anything – rewards, blessings, eternal life, etc. Rather, He wants us to love Him enough that we want to obey Him. That should be our goal. That is the ideal. If we do not keep the ideal before us, we do not know what we are trying to attain.

We should think of ourselves not as being sinless but as being toddlers, heading for the held-out hands of a loving daddy who will give us whatever help we need and desire. If we do not have God's ideal in front of us as a goal, we will be like a neglected child who is left in a crib all day and not helped to learn how to walk. Like toddlers, we will stumble and fall – we will not be perfect. But God will help us back up and we can again aim for the ideal of His holiness. The toddler does not give up because he falls, but rejoices in the steps taken and is exuberant even in small accomplishments. As we mature in God, we should stumble less, but even adults sometimes fall down. We can be sure that Satan is ready to trip us up any time he can. Yet no matter how many times we sin, our loving Father is always there to pick us up and help us get started in the right direction again.

When we allow ourselves to lose sight of God's standards, we are the ones who suffer the most. Our lives tend to fall apart when we try to follow what others are doing or what we think would be good to do. We need to keep His high ideals before us. We need to pray constantly that God will help us, then do our best to follow Him. God wants what is best for us. The happiest, most fulfilling life we can live is doing what is right and avoiding what is wrong. God's way is always the best way.

Sometimes we feel that we cannot live up to the expectations God has for us. We feel that we should be able to get by with less. "Surely it is not necessary to do EVERYTHING God wants," we think.

However, we should notice that nowhere in the Bible does God say, "I know I have set a high standard of holiness and obedience for you, and I understand that you cannot always live up to my standards. Therefore, just do as much as makes you comfortable. I'll overlook anything and everything, just as long as what you do makes you happy. Everything will come out in the wash and will be okay in the end. I love you too much to punish you even if you do something wrong or if you do not do what is right." That might be what we wish God says or what some of us seem to understand God to say, but it is not so!

Instead God sets high standards for us and wants us to do the best we can to live up to those standards in order for us to honor Him. Numbers 20 tells the story of Moses' striking the rock in order to quench the thirst of the Israelites wandering in the desert. God told Moses exactly what to do, and Moses started out following His commands; however, somewhere along the way, Moses deviated from what God said. Whether Moses' sin was in what he said or what he did, we are not sure. However, in explaining the significance of his sin, God said to Moses in Numbers 20:12, "Because you did not trust in me enough to honor me as holy in the sight of the Israelites, you will not bring this community into the land I give them."

In Deuteronomy 32:51 God explained again the reason for punishing Moses: "[B]ecause ... you broke faith with me in the presence of the Israelites at the waters of Meribah Kadesh in the Desert of Zin and because you did not uphold my holiness among the Israelites." In this instance, Moses did not trust God enough to honor Him by obeying Him, and thus denied His holiness.

It seems that the basis of Moses' sin was that he did not honor God. How do we honor God? Perhaps looking at one of the Ten Commandments will help us understand. "Honor your father and your mother" (Exodus 20:12). When children honor their parents, they listen to them, pay attention to them, and follow the instructions of the parents. They obey them. They do not do things that are against the principles taught them by their parents. This is also the way we honor God. When we listen to Him, pay attention to what He says, and follow His instructions, we show to others that we trust in God and believe that His way is the best way for us and for everyone. We show that His way is the honorable way, the way of integrity. God wants us to be pure in all aspects of our lives, and we bring honor to Him and uphold His holiness when we try to live worthily according to His principles.

Conclusion

Why bother trying to live a worthy life? Because it is God's way, and God's way is always the best way. Once we have decided that we want to do things His way, many decisions are already made for us. His way is better and easier. On the surface, living a worthy life may appear to be more difficult, but it really is not because God is with us and helps us. With time and experience in following God's way, the blessings become more evident.

It is not that if we just trust God, life will be perfect, easy, happy-go-lucky, trouble free, pain free, worry free, care free, with no problems and no hassles. Rather, it is that with God's help we can have the best quality of life possible on this earth. We will have the strength to go on. We will have the guidance we need to make our decisions, to know which way to turn. He gives us the inner strength that makes all the difference in the world. It is hard for people who do not know God and do not trust Him to manage their lives. But with God's help we can overcome anything the devil can throw at us.

Everything we do must fit into the framework of a worthy life. Our lives will never be what God wants them to be unless we are totally, completely and joyfully committed to obeying Him from the heart. Only then will we be truly free to live worthy lives in His service. It is not so much that we just do what God wants us to do, but that we become essentially obedient people, submissive to God as we try to have the mind of Christ and be one with Him.

When we are truly aware of the holiness and glory of God, we will feel the reverent and holy awe that is appropriate to His magnificence. We need to be aware of the presence of God in our lives, in our hearts, in our beings, so that we will live a life worthy of His presence at all times. There is nothing so beautiful in this world as living the way God intends.

Discussion Questions

1. Sometimes you may feel that the fog of your life is so thick that God's presence cannot penetrate it. In what ways does this feeling fail to represent the true situation? Compare this to the sun making itself felt even through thick clouds.

2. Describe a time in your life when you strongly felt God's presence with you. How did this affect your actions? How does God's presence help you to live worthily? In what ways does God's presence give you strength?

3. What does the phrase, "God will take care of you," mean to you? How will He take care of you? What will He do for you?

4. What kind of peace can you have when God is with you? What experiences have you had that illustrate the presence of the peace of God in your life?

5. How can a person who is surrounded with the problems and the stress of life find joy in living? How would you describe this kind of joy?

6. Did Paul think living the Christian life was worth all the terrible things that happened to him? How do you know? Relate Paul's thinking on this subject to your life.

7. What experiences have you had in your life that illustrate the concept that living the Christian life really is worthwhile, really the best way? In what areas of your life can you see that God's way is best? How does this knowledge affect the way you live?

8. What are some of the blessings you receive as you try to live your life in a worthy way for the Lord? Can you find scriptures that relate to these?

9. How do you feel about the high standards that God has set for you? Why do you think He insists upon these

standards? Do such high standards discourage you, or do they challenge the best that is in you? What is the proper response to feelings of discouragement?

10. What do you see in your life that you need to change in order to live a worthy life? How can you make these changes?

11. What can you do to honor God and His holiness in your life?

Scripture Index